"How lucky we are that the greatest raconteur in the Bluegrass has now told its greatest story—which just happens to be his own. He has done so with all the courage, humor and poetic sense that sustained his captivating triumph against the odds."

—CHRIS MCGRATH, author of *Mr. Darley's Arabian*

"A compelling and inspiring story of how one can reach within himself to conquer the demons and create a life of success and happiness."

—TED BASSETT, American Thoroughbred Industry Ambassador

"Arthur Hancock is a born storyteller and the one uncorked here is part big-hearted look at one of the Bluegrass's first families, and part autobiography of a songwriter of heartbreaks who overcame them, a book soaked in whiskey and passion of a first-rate horseman."

—JOE DRAPE, New York Times journalist and bestselling author

"A riveting and well-written history."

—GEORGE W. STRAWBRIDGE JR., Augustin Stable, award winning owner and breeder

"Hancock's life story is poignantly uplifting, rollicking, triumphant and persistently compelling on every page."

—JIM SQUIRES, Pulitzer Prize-winning journalist

"A book about friendship and the magnetism of the horses in the Sport of Kings."

—ALEC HEAD, Legendary French owner, breeder and trainer

DARK HORSES

A Memoir of Redemption

Arthur B. Hancock III

Dark Horses

Copyright ©2024 by Arthur Hancock

Published by Stone Publishing, LLC
ArthurHancock.com

Hardcover ISBN: 979-8-9916690-0-9

Paperback ISBN: 979-8-9916690-1-6

eISBN: 979-8-9916690-2-3

Cover and Interior Design: GKS Creative

Copyediting and Proofreading: Monti Shalosky

Project Management: The Cadence Group

For Mama and Daddy,

my wife Staci, our children,

and all of the horses.

Contents

With my father, grandfather, and our dog Spot in the library at Claiborne House – Hancock Family Photo

PART ONE

Grandaddy in his three-piece suit – Ed Weddle Photo

CHAPTER 1

The Hancocks

EVEN THE MEMORY of my grandfather Arthur Boyd Hancock Sr. is imposing. He was six foot six inches tall, grand indeed in his three-piece suit. A gentleman of his time, he had a fine formal education from Johns Hopkins University and the University of Chicago. Granddaddy always had a chauffeur, and we would go through the mares and foals together. I used to open gates for him as we drove through the pastures of Claiborne Farm. He paid me ten cents a gate. I still remember my father, Arthur Boyd Hancock Jr., who only paid a nickel, saying to him that he was going to spoil me by paying too much.

They both schooled me from an early age so that one day I could follow their footsteps in the Thoroughbred dynasty they had created. Both my grandfather and father would point out different characteristics of the horses and give me tips about how they should look and how to judge them. In 1936, my grandfather imported the great European stallion Blenheim to Kentucky. One day we were riding through the mares and foals and in his thick Virginia accent, he said,

"Grandson, you see how all these Blenheim foals look like they've been cut out with a cookie cuttah?" He was pointing out to me that they all looked the same in a certain way. He said that was a very good sign for a stallion when he "stamped" his foals like Blenheim did, and it generally meant he would be a good sire.

My grandfather was said to have been very strict and hard on my father, but he was very loving and forgiving toward me. I remember him giving me a miniature filling station with gas pumps and cars, and a cowboy outfit with twin pistols and a colorful vest. Those who knew him said this was very uncharacteristic for a man who had been extremely frugal, very businesslike, and quite strict with everyone else all his life. Mama always said that for as long as he was alive, he never wanted to give my father any credit for Claiborne's accomplishments.

Father and son, Grandaddy and Daddy at the Claiborne office – Keeneland Library Meadors Collection

The only time I ever really saw this side of him is one of my earliest recollections, when I was a small boy about the age of four. The Claiborne filly named Bluegrass had won the prestigious Kentucky Oaks in 1947, and I remember my father coming home that same evening from Churchill Downs in a most exuberant and euphoric mood.

He dropped my mother off at Claiborne House and told me to come with him to "tell Dad about the great victory." We drove to "the boss's house" as my father called it—a stately home in the middle of Paris, Kentucky—and went upstairs where my grandfather was sitting in a large, comfortable chair with a blanket over his legs. His extra-long cane, needed by a man so tall, was propped at his feet.

By this time, he was seventy-two and a stroke hadn't left him in the best of health. It had affected his speech and he spoke very slowly and with difficulty.

With a legacy of superb horsemanship from his father, the "Captain" Richard J. Hancock, he had laid what much of the world considered to be the cornerstone of America's Thoroughbred industry. Now in poor health, along with his name, he was about to grudgingly pass Claiborne Farm to his descendants.

My father was holding my hand when we walked in the room. He was all smiles and very cheerful. He said, "Dad, Dad, my filly won the Kentucky Oaks today!"

Being naturally unhappy in his current condition, my grandfather had a depressed and frustrated frown on his face. He reached down and grabbed the long cane that supported his lengthy frame, raised it, and tried to hook it around Daddy's neck. "My filly," he growled. "My filly!"

His only son would be known far and wide for most of his life as "Bull" Hancock—and for good reason, too. Daddy had the presence of one and sometimes the behavior. He earned his nickname when he was a student at Princeton by volunteering to climb in the ring with a carnival attraction brawler who was offering fifty dollars to anyone who could last three rounds or knock him down. Daddy floored him with one huge right fist within the first minute.

He carried this name all his life and was every bit as fierce, quick-tempered, and strong as it implied. A prominent horse racing journalist once described him as "the biggest man, physically speaking, in the Thoroughbred industry of his day . . ." At six foot two and 230 pounds, he looked like a giant to me when I was a child—and with his booming voice when angry, sounded like one. When he walked into a room, he had an aura and a presence about him.

When I was a little boy, I had terrible asthma, and he thought I might be conjuring it up in some way to get attention from my mother. I was a bed wetter as well and to prevent this, I got a spanking every morning until it was evident that this wasn't going to help. I always said "yes, sir" and "yes, ma'am" when answering. Once I forgot it, accidentally saying "nope" several times, and I got a licking for that, too.

The first time I remember my father ever getting really mad at me was one Sunday afternoon in the spring of 1949 when I was six. We went riding in the car through those beautiful, lush bluegrass fields to look at the horses. I was in the back seat with my sister, Clay, and our mother was up front.

Daddy kept driving around and around in circles looking at different foals and mares and constantly commenting on them in terms I really didn't understand. To me, it was very boring. I had a new toy John Deere tractor and I wanted to go home and play with it in the sand pile. After a while, I blurted out, "I don't want to look at these stupid old horses all day."

Daddy wheeled around like he was going to hit me, pale blue eyes glaring. Quivering with emotion and in a loud voice, he pointed his finger at me and sternly said, "Don't you ever, ever say anything bad about these horses again. Do you understand me? They give us our livelihood and talking bad about them is the same thing as the dog that bites the hand that feeds it."

It really frightened me and took me off guard. All I could manage in response was a meek "yes, sir." My mother immediately got mad, and I remember her saying, "Bull, he's just a little boy." Looking back on that day years later, I came to understand what was impossible for me then. For nearly a hundred years, Hancock men had been successfully inspecting and evaluating horses for a living in a risky, unforgiving business. It was the first of many early lessons my father tried to teach me that had been passed down through the years. One of his favorite sayings was "shirtsleeves to shirtsleeves in three generations."

My father was a great and good man, sometimes sensitive and kind, who, on the other hand, brooked no foolishness from his children if we crossed him. His retribution was swift and harsh. And, unfortunately for me, I would never let up. Once he told me, "You should go into politics because you are the damnedest agitator I ever met."

The same turf writer who called Bull Hancock the "biggest man" physically also wrote that he "towered over his contemporaries in professional ability and the dominance of his personality."

When he died in 1972, *The New York Times* decreed him the world's leading breeder of Thoroughbred horses. In the years he ran Claiborne, the farm raised thirty-two world champions sired by some of the most famous stallions in the history of the breed. He was a bigger-than-life figure. From my first days as a child reading about the horse business, Arthur Boyd Hancock Jr. was the moral equivalent of reading about George Patton or John Wayne—Bull Hancock of Claiborne Farm—a legend, a hero, my father.

Most likely, whatever made him climb into the carnival ring with a professional fighter is what drove him in the breeding business. In any endeavor, he was bold and ferocious.

My Father and the famous Phipps family stallion Buckpasser – John Noye Photo

The night after the Kentucky Derby in 1953, when my father and Harry Guggenheim came back to Claiborne House, they were both very excited and in a jovial frame of mind. And no wonder—Mr. Guggenheim's horse, Dark Star, had just defeated the great Native Dancer that afternoon in one of the biggest Derby upsets of all time.

Harry Guggenheim was one of the most prominent men in America, quite wealthy and very well politically connected. He was a gentleman. I was only ten years old, but he was always nice to me, and I liked him very much. At the time, he was Claiborne's best client. He had a big racing stable, Cain Hoy, and he was a member of the syndicate in the purchase of Nasrullah to stand at Claiborne. He had four other stallions at the farm, Dark Star, Dead Ahead, Bald Eagle, and Turn-to.

My father had made Turn-to one of the leading stallions in America, and he was very proud of this fact. For each stallion that stood at Claiborne, the farm received four breeding rights a year for managing him. These breeding rights created a large stream of revenue.

Mr. Guggenheim also had roughly thirty mares, twenty-five yearlings, and twenty-two foals at the farm. This was a very lucrative association for my father as well as for Claiborne. The board bills were enormous, and it was a feather in the cap of anyone to be associated with such a well-known and prominent man.

We were just about to have dinner one night when the phone rang, and it was Mr. Guggenheim. I don't know exactly what was said during that call, but in so many words he told my father that the farm was only going to get three breeding rights in Turn-to for the coming breeding season, because he had given one of Claiborne's four annual seasons to a very important unnamed friend.

I heard my father say in a stern voice, "Harry, that was not our agreement. That breeding right belongs to Claiborne and it is going to stay with Claiborne." Obviously upset and angry, he slammed the phone down.

My father and Mr. Guggenheim – Keeneland Library Collection

Nathan, a jockey-sized black man with a keen sense of humor and drama, came in and announced that dinner was ready in the dining room. He was Mama's right hand around the house and was like a member of the family for more than twenty years. My mother asked what in the world was going on. Daddy didn't say a word, which was very unlike him. A deep simmering rage had taken possession of his normally outgoing and outspoken personality.

After a couple of courses, the phone rang again. Nathan came back in the dining room and said, "It's Mr. Guggenheim."

Daddy told Nathan to tell him that he was having his dinner and would call him in the morning. Nathan went back and told Mr. Guggenheim but returned almost immediately to get my father because the caller had insisted "this couldn't wait."

The next thing I heard was my father roaring, "If that's the way you want it, the best thing for you to do is get your horses off this farm by sundown tomorrow, and if they aren't out of here by sundown, so help me God, I will turn every one of 'em out on the highway."

Next morning, there were vans lined up from the Claiborne office all the way out to the highway waiting to pick up the multitude of horses Mr. Guggenheim had at the farm. Every van owned by the Van Gorp Van Company was there waiting.

The horses were all sent to the big rival of Claiborne at that time, Spendthrift Farm, owned by Leslie Combs. It was said by people that Mr. Combs was ecstatic and was like the cat who had just eaten the canary.

Years later, my father recalled the episode with obvious satisfaction that "Leslie Combs never raised Mr. Guggenheim another good horse!"

From that time on, Spendthrift, Claiborne, and all the other stallion farms made sure that their stallion syndication agreements were in writing and drawn up by a good attorney.

The horse business is really a people business and always has been. Once, the great trainer Horatio Luro said, "Training the horses is easy, training the owners is hard."

As I grew up at beautiful and historic Claiborne House, with four large columns in the front, a big, manicured lawn and a swimming pool, from time to time there would be visitors from all over the world, and there would be some big dinner parties and raucous gatherings.

This brought the members of my family into contact with some of the most interesting, celebrated, and accomplished people in the world, including financiers, bankers, stockbrokers, and titans of industry.

Mama and Daddy in Palm Beach – Keeneland Library Collection

Besides the prominent Mr. Guggenheim, there was movie mogul Louis B. Mayer; car rental pioneer John Hertz; William Woodward Sr., heir to the Hanover National Bank fortune; Marshall Field, the newspaper and retail titan from Chicago; Texas oilman Bunker Hunt; and the two men who would ultimately and profoundly impact the direction of my life, investment banker Ogden Phipps, and William Haggin Perry, whose family helped found the Keeneland Association.

Sometimes, they also included many of my parents' friends from around Bourbon County. They were the wildest ones and whenever they would come over, the party usually lasted past midnight. A lot of tales were told, and a lot of good bourbon whiskey was drunk beside a blazing fire in the living room at Claiborne House.

When I was about eight years old, I had five lovely goldfish, each of whom I had named and whom I loved dearly. Every day, I fed them and watched them as they gleefully glided through the water playing with one another and trying to be the first one to get to the feed that I would meticulously give them. They were my beloved pets; they were my friends.

One rainy night, my parents had a gathering of their Bourbon County friends, and as usual, the party really got rolling after dinner. I remember waking up in my room above them about midnight and hearing somebody saying, "Goddamn, I can feel the sons of bitches jumping around . . ."

I thought that was rather strange, but I didn't think much about it and went right back to sleep.

The next morning, when I came down and walked into the living room, the ashtrays were full of cigarette butts and short and tall glasses with the Claiborne racing silks engraved on them were strewn all around the room. I turned to the table to say good morning to my goldfish friends.

They were all gone.

I couldn't believe it. In a heartbroken panic, I ran looking for my mother who was in the kitchen having a cup of coffee. With tears in my eyes and fear in my heart, I said, "Mama, Mama, where are my little goldfish?"

With a look of gravity, regret, and pity in her sad blue eyes, she solemnly put her hands on my shoulders and said, in her deep Southern accent, "Ahhthuh, Mistuh Talbot ate yo' goldfish."

In early September of 1957, I was in a field of two dozen armed men on a hillside in Kentucky, just a kid getting ready to be one of them someday. I was fourteen going on twenty-five.

The afternoon sun was hot enough to fry an egg on the hood of a pickup truck. Dove season had just opened in Kentucky. A time-honored Kentucky ritual, "dove shoots" are where friends, neighbors, and out-of-town guests gather in a farmer's field of millet or plowed-under sunflowers to tell stories, shoot doves, and just have a big time.

This was not my first dove shoot, but it was the first time I ever tried putting peroxide in my hair in a cornfield. A couple of days earlier, I had gone to Ardery's Drug Store and bought some black dye for the good and simple reason that I wanted to look like Elvis Presley and Ricky Nelson. That night, I rubbed it in my hair and woke up the next morning with solid jet-black locks. Still too young to shave, I had let my hair grow long in front of my ears so I could pull it down to make it look like real sideburns.

Daddy didn't see me that morning but came in late in the afternoon just in time for dinner. When I strolled in with my new look, he stared at my hair combed back on the sides with the pulled-down imitation sideburns, and said in his Bourbon County accent, "Oh my God! Anybody who dyes their hair black has got to be a sissy and there's absolutely no question about that."

It really hurt my feelings, and I emotionally assured him that I was not. My mother chimed in, "Bull, that was the meanest thing I evuh heard anybody say to a young boy."

The dove shoot, at Quentin Walker's 2,000-acre farm the following afternoon, was typical for the times, by invitation only and attended by the large landowners in Bourbon County, a couple of judges, and my father's best friends. As the oldest son of one of the country's most prominent Thoroughbred horse breeders, I was expected to be present and presentable. But that morning I went back to Ardery's and bought a bottle of hydrogen peroxide, which I took with me to the dove field. My newly blackened hair was safely hidden under my camouflaged hunting hat.

Moses, who worked for Quentin, drove the hunters to their designated shooting spots and fortunately dropped me off down by a little stream next to a cornfield, where I took off my hat and alternated rubbing peroxide in my hair and wetting it in the stream. By the time I got my dove limit and walked back up the hill and into the circle of hunters including my father and his prominent peers, the sun-driven peroxide had turned my Elvis hair into a gleaming shade of blond.

Among the gathered guests were the usual roughhewn and tough Kentuckians and several men who had served in World War II under General Patton. One of them, Colonel Walter Hillenmeyer, knew Patton personally. He was entertaining the group with a story he had witnessed on the outskirts of Paris, France when he was among the officers who approached General Patton seeking permission to go into the city that night.

As he told the story: "We were standing stiffly at attention when the general said, 'At ease, boys, what's on your mind?' As we all relaxed a bit, I said, 'General Patton, Sir, we are all here to request permission to enter the city tonight.'

'Why in the hell do you want to go into Paris? You boys want to go in there and get a little, don't you?'

When we all replied, 'Affirmative, Sir,' General Patton said, 'Permission granted, boys. I am a firm believer that if a man won't fuck, he won't fight!'"

As the laughter settled into the hillside, my father caught sight of his newly blond son and stood up, amused and aghast, from the bed of a pickup truck where he had been sitting. He took one look at me and sarcastically said, "Now I know damn well you're a sissy."

His friend, Doug Parrish, a man so strong he could pick up the front of a tractor, said to my father, "Bull, don't be so hard on him. You know, the apple don't fall too far from the tree."

My father smiled and replied, "That is generally true, but in his case, it rolled down the goddamned hill."

With trimmed sideburns and dyed black hair – Hancock Family Photo

My father's temper was legendary. On a warm spring night in the late 1960s, he got a call from the foaling barn. They told him his mare Continue was going to foal very shortly. Daddy told me to come with him if I wanted to see her deliver her foal and we got in the car.

His chief ambition in life—like mine became—was to win the Kentucky Derby. On the way to the barn, Daddy told me that if we could get a colt out of Continue, he would be a prime candidate to win the Derby. She was extremely well bred and was in foal to the great horse Forli.

When we got to the barn, the mare was in heavy labor, and it wasn't long before she delivered her baby. Daddy said to Jimmy Christopher, who was in charge, "Whatcha got, Jimmy?"

When Jimmy replied, "It's a filly, Mr. Hancock," my father kicked the water bucket over and said, "Goddammit, all I get are fuckin' fillies. I'll never win the goddamned Derby. The Lord has got his finger pointed at me."

After he furiously stormed around the barn for a couple of minutes, he gathered himself, walked back to the stall and said, "Is she okay, Jimmy?"

Jimmy gently raised her head from the straw and said, "She's just got one eye, Mr. Hancock."

I saw it myself. There was just a layer of skin where there was supposed to be an eye.

You would have thought that my father was going to literally explode. He kicked the metal feed tub, which had been removed from the stall, all the way up into the air and it clanked eerily down the barn hall on the blacktop, shattering the silence, followed by what sounded like a muffled roar mixed with a sob. He then turned to me and said, "Get in the goddamned car."

That little filly was eventually named Tuerta, which means one eye in Spanish. Like a lot of other imperfect creatures, equine and human, she turned out to be a child of destiny and a good lesson for me. Her son Swale became the Derby winner my father had always dreamed about. But when Swale won The Kentucky Derby in 1984, my father had been dead for twelve years.

Not long after my dyed-hair episode had embarrassed my father before his friends in the dove field, I was sent to the Woodberry Forest Boarding School in Orange, Virginia where he had gone and had distinguished himself athletically.

When I was in the fourth form (tenth grade) at Woodberry, I got in a fight with my roommate and accidentally hit the bedpost of the bunk bed. The pain in my little finger was horrendous, and an X-ray showed that my knuckle had migrated two inches from its normal position toward my wrist.

On the train to see an orthopedic surgeon in Charlottesville, I met a strange-looking man with shoulder length white hair and piercing blue eyes who looked out of place by the way he was dressed and how he walked.

The train was somewhat crowded, and he sat down in the vacant seat next to me. When he learned that the right hand I was holding up next to my chest had been injured in a fist fight, he said, "This country round heah seen a whole lotta fittin'. I membuh the old Civil Wahhh."

I could hardly believe him. "You remember the Civil War?" I asked.

"I membuh it wale. I was just a little small boy back then, but you don't nevuhh fuhgit them times."

I said, "Were the Yankees mean?"

He said, "No, they give us chillen candy. But thuh ole people didn't like 'em much. They was lines of blue as fuhh as you could see when they come thu heahh . . . They was rough on evuhbody, but it got bettuh as the yeeahhs went on."

He said he was 101 years old, born in 1856. I sat there amazed at what had just happened. I had touched the Civil War. If I'd had the presence of mind, I would have asked him if he had ever met or heard of a man in Charlottesville called "The Captain"—the rank my great-grandfather had held in the Army of Northern Virginia.

Richard Johnson Hancock fought for four years in the Civil War. He became a prisoner after being wounded at the third battle of Winchester on September 19, 1864. Before he could be shipped to a northern prisoner of war camp, he escaped with the help of two female Southern sympathizers. Later, he was wounded at Manassas, and lastly at Gettysburg from where he was taken on a mule-drawn ambulance back to Charlottesville. There, he met and married my great-grandmother, Thomasia Overton Harris, and became the master of Ellerslie, a magnificent farm near Charlottesville where he developed an extraordinary skill as a horseman.

Both "The Captain" and my grandfather married lovely, pedigreed women who eventually inherited the most valuable treasure of their times—hundreds and hundreds of acres of beautiful, rich Virginia and Kentucky farmland perfect for raising all manner of crops, including fine horses.

Arthur Boyd Hancock Sr., fourth son of Captain Hancock and already the manager of the family's Virginia farm, met my grandmother Nancy Clay when he came to Kentucky to judge a horseshow. After their courtship, they married and moved from Virginia to settle in Bourbon County in 1915 where they developed the thirteen hundred acres she had inherited. The name Claiborne was chosen to reflect upon one of Kentucky's oldest and most famous families, the Clays, of which my grandmother was a descendant. Among her distant cousins and kinfolk were the

My great-grandfather, Captain
Richard Johnson Hancock –
Hancock Family Photo

With Civil War Comrades who had
served with him in the Army of Northern
Virginia. Captain Hancock, with cane,
was still recovering from a wound
suffered during a night attack on
Cemetary Ridge at Gettysburg
– Hancock Family Photo

abolitionist Cassius Clay, Ambassador to Russia, and the renowned Kentucky statesman, Henry Clay.

My father followed in his forefathers' footsteps when he married Waddell Walker, daughter of Nashville's most prominent and respected attorney. Mama spoke with a soft Old South accent and, to me, was the classic southern belle, who could have walked out of *Gone with the Wind*.

The elegant lifestyle of old Virginia wealth, along with the legacy of military discipline and aversion to foolishness that Richard Hancock took from his four long years in the war, were passed along from generation to generation.

My grandfather said that Captain Hancock had treated all his sons "like the very troops he commanded during the war." This same regimen of restrained praise and strict discipline was passed on to my father, and eventually to me.

My table had been set by the three of them, all men of high confidence, great strength, hot temper, and good fortune. From the time I was a small boy, I knew I was expected to eventually run Claiborne and carry on the great tradition they had established.

In the 1920s, when my Grandfather Hancock was importing the stallion Sir Gallahad III from the French, my maternal great-grandfather, Judge Seth M. Walker Sr., was Speaker of the Tennessee House of Representatives, where he led a losing fight to oppose ratification of the Nineteenth Amendment that guaranteed women's right to vote. He lost that fight by a single vote and Tennessee became the crucial thirty-sixth state needed for ratification, assuring him a controversial place in history.

His son, Seth M. Walker Jr. was also elected to the Tennessee House and is arguably as legendary in the legal circles of Nashville as my Grandfather Hancock was in the Thoroughbred horse industry. He passed away in 1951. More than a half-century after his death, the consensus of a Nashville Bar Association history seminar was that he was the most admired and respected Nashville attorney in the twentieth century. Two other legal titans of the time, my uncle John J. Hooker Sr. and the legendary Jack Norman said that Seth Walker was the best lawyer they ever met and that they had patterned their careers after his.

As Arthur B. Hancock III, I was heir to the strong opinions and the fierce independent natures of all of these men. All through my life, this could land me in hot water—but it also meant that I would never, ever give up.

CHAPTER 2

Bulldogs and Lambs

SOMETIMES I WONDER now how it happened that bulldogs with their unpredictable violent nature seemed to be as common to life at Claiborne in those days as beautiful horses, pet piglets, and gentle little lambs.

It cannot be as simple as my father's nickname but who knows? I think Daddy liked them because they were tough. The English used to fight them and generally no other breed of dog could beat them. Daddy used to talk about how they would start at the leg and bite by bite change grips until they worked up to the neck for the kill.

A dog named Buck Buck was the first bulldog I remember. Daddy loved that dog but a neighbor who owned sheep killed him while Daddy was in Saratoga and my mother decided not to say anything to him until he returned. But he found out about it somehow when he called home to check on the horses. It was all she could do to talk him out of coming home immediately.

When he got back to the farm, I remember her telling him to take a deep breath and think about all he had to lose before confronting the man who shot his dog. I think Daddy was aware of the terrible power of his temper. I remember him saying, "It was a good thing I was in Saratoga, because if I'd been home, I'd have killed him, sure as hell."

⊂━━━⊃

My sister Clay had a burley bulldog named Mike, who repeatedly ignited Daddy. One night, he stole and ate four large New York strip steaks Daddy had stashed atop the refrigerator and planned to grill for the family. Daddy flew into a rage and went after Mike, who ran around the kitchen table twice and then headed out into the hall with my father right behind him cursing and kicking at him.

Luckily for Mike, the screen door leading to the back steps was not latched. When Mike hit it at full speed, it flew open, and he escaped. We had a supper of bread, salad, and stewed tomatoes, and an evening of listening to Daddy wonder how in the hell that sonofabitch could have leapt onto the counter, and then onto the refrigerator.

It was not long thereafter that Mike rode with us one warm September morning to the training track at Xalapa Farm, with my sister Clay and me in Daddy's new station wagon, to see a dozen yearlings coming out from the barn. We were going to watch the set from inside an octagonal-shaped viewing stand in the center of the racetrack where you could see the horses circling around. We left Mike in the car, unfortunately with the windows rolled up.

After the horses finished galloping, we walked back to the car. There were some very well-bred colts in the set, and Daddy had high hopes that one of them could possibly be his Kentucky Derby winner one day.

As we approached the car, we could hear yelping and whimpering. The windshield and all the windows were totally steamed up. When

Daddy opened the door, a frantic, panicked, saliva-covered bulldog jumped out, panting like he was breathing his last breath.

My father bellowed a shriek that was a raw mixture of pain and rage. As he cursed, I opened the passenger door. I was flabbergasted.

The steering wheel was bent in several places with big teeth marks all over it. The two visors had been ripped to shreds. The ceiling cloth had been torn all to pieces and was hanging down, and the beautiful leather seats were ripped and covered in saliva and froth. The panel under the windshield had four large bites taken out of it like it was a piece of cake.

When I saw the carnage, I had to bite my tongue to keep from laughing. Daddy, in his fit of rage, kept sobbing and repeating, "You goddamn sonofabitch. You dirty no-good sonofabitch. Oh goddamn! Has anybody got a gun? Please, has anybody got a goddamn gun?" Mike had eaten his steaks and now had torn up his car!

All the while, he was cursing the dog and chasing him around and around the car trying to kick him. Mike retreated back into the car he had just shredded and cowered in what remained of the back seat.

Our yearling manager, John Sosby, was visibly shaken. The exercise riders were shocked and the old timers at Claiborne still talk about it to this day. Everybody said they had never, ever seen a man get so mad. Daddy growled at Sosby, "Get in the car, take it to the dealer, and trade it off."

We took Sosby's truck and drove it back to Claiborne House and not a word was said the whole way home. My shoulders were heaving every couple of minutes, and I still had to bite my tongue, smothering laughter that I knew would turn Daddy's rage on me.

Mike was a survivor. But not all of our dogs were so lucky. On Christmas morning, when I was nineteen, a phone call interrupted our breakfast and I answered to hear a sheep man on a farm two miles away ranting and raving about shooting a dog.

I asked him what in the hell he was talking about.

"I caught 'em both in my barn. I blowed a hole in the white one and sicced my dogs on the other'n! They tore his ass all to pieces. I knowed the dogs was yourn 'cause I got their collars."

Both were American Bulldogs who came to the same violent end as Buck Buck, and for the same persistent and uncontrollable bad behavior—getting into the sheep. Maxine belonged to my sister, Dell, who was only nine, and Butch belonged to my brother, Seth, who was just twelve. Even now, they will tell you that was the most horrible and heartbreaking Christmas they have ever been through.

With little brother Seth and my bulldog Mac looking at a yearling – Hancock Family Photo

COUNTRY BOY

Country Boy, goin' fishin'
Country boy, wild and free
Country boy, how I'm wishin'
To be the country boy I used to be

Country boy, in the meadow
Country boy, by the stream
Country boy, through the shadow
A little country boy in a country dream

Play all day with my old dog Mac
Roam the farm to the rundown shack
I'd give my soul to journey back
And be like you are now

This busy life has got me goin'
There's so little time for me
The more I live, the more I'm knowin'
This uptown livin' ain't the life for me

I wanna be out there just me and God
Go barefooted in the grassy sod
Steal away with my fishin' rod
And be like you are now

Country boy, goin' fishin'
Country boy, wild and free
Country boy, how I'm wishin'
To be the country boy I used to be

When I was twelve years old, I had a wonderful English Bulldog named Mac. We were truly soulmates. Before I went away to prep school, I went to the Paris City School where I made several good friends. Back then, boys often played marbles, a game on the ground where a "shooter" flicks one marble into a circle of others aiming to knock one outside. When I played, one boy who didn't like me at all would come up and kick the marbles and say that they were for sissies.

He had perceived me to be a spoiled brat from a wealthy family, and though only half right, had nicknamed me Little Lord Fauntleroy. Sometimes, when Charlton Brooks, a quiet and kind man who drove for my parents, came to pick me up after school, the bully would say, "Look, here comes Fauntleroy's houseboy to pick him up."

One day, when we were riding on a merry-go-round, the bully walked up and said he was gonna whip anybody's ass who was still on it in one minute. Of course, everybody got off but me. He came over and jerked me off the merry-go-round into the dust and everybody laughed. Somebody said, "Fauntleroy bites the dust."

Although he was in the fifth grade with me, he could whip boys that were in the seventh and eighth grade. Nobody messed with this boy. Everyone, it seemed, steered clear of him. I told my father about him, and he said, "Son, let me tell you what to do. The next time he bothers you, hit him as hard as you can right square in the nose and mouth, and even though you may get your ass whipped, he will leave you alone from then on."

As was often the case in those days, I thought about following my father's advice and even laid awake at night anguishing over it. I had seen what this bully had done to some of the other kids. He was mean, and when he got mad, there was no telling what he would do to you.

I had a better idea. I had trained my bulldog Mac to attack on command. I had read in a book that a good way to make a dog aggressive was to emit a shrill shriek and point to whatever you wanted him to jump on. And it worked. He would not hesitate when I gave him the signal.

Mac had already proven that he was somewhat ferocious. On Christmas Eve, he had attacked and ripped the red coat off Santa Claus being played by Mr. Mastin, who at my mother's invitation, had come barging in the front door repeatedly bellowing, "Ho-ho-ho." I had to pull Mac, snapping and snarling, away from Santa just as he snagged a section of his fake beard inches from his throat. A shaken Santa badly needed and immediately received a stiff double shot of Jack Daniels!

One night after I went to bed and was fretting about how to deal with the bully, the idea occurred to me that if I could get him to come out to the farm, I would sic Mac on him. He had singled me out. I couldn't go on being humiliated and treated like dirt. I was constantly walking on eggshells.

The next time he teased me at school, I said, "I can't help it that I was born with money and a farm, any more than you can help it you were born without them, and I don't know why you should hate me for that. Why don't you come out and play with me and see our farm? Maybe you won't feel so hateful and mean toward me."

That sort of took him off guard and he didn't say anything, but a couple of days later, I asked him again and he agreed to come out and visit after school one afternoon. I remember him telling me that just because he was coming out to the farm didn't mean he was going to like me, and that it might make him hate me more, in which case he was really going to tear my ass up.

My mother came to pick us up that afternoon. She politely said hello to the bully, and we had a nice drive and conversation back out to Claiborne. When we got there, I said that I would get my dog and we would take a hike through the farm to show him around.

We were down by the creek looking for snakes under rocks when I decided the moment of truth had finally arrived. I said to him, "You have made me miserable at school and picked on me for the last two months and I'm not gonna take it anymore. You're gonna die."

Then I issued my shrill shriek and pointed my finger at him. Mac responded accordingly. He jumped and caught him by the jacket and ripped off half of the sleeve. We were standing by a water gap, and in about two seconds, the bully went up the fence and onto the top of the concrete abutment. By this time, Mac was trying to jump up and grab him.

Mac could actually climb trees, and he was figuring out how to use the fence with a running start and almost get up to the top of the gap. He was snarling and snapping his teeth as he attempted to bite the bully's legs.

I was enjoying this immensely, and all the emotion and anxiety that had built up in me was finally coming out. Revenge was so sweet. But then I looked up and saw the bully standing up there shaking and trembling with tears in his eyes.

He pleaded with me to stop the dog. "I'm so sorry I've been mean to you and I swear to God, I'll never treat you bad again. Please get him off," he begged. "Arthur, please call him off."

I did. And the bully got down from the water gap and we shook hands and went back up to the house. I told him that if he ever bothered me again, I would bring the dog to school with me. About that time, my father drove up and said, "Son, what happened to your jacket?"

Before he could answer, I did. "Daddy, Mac was playing with him and tore his sleeve."

My father said he was sorry and that never should have happened to a guest at Claiborne. It wasn't right, he said, to visit a place and have the dog ruin your coat. He gave him some money and told him to get himself a new one. The bully was happy.

Strangely enough, after that, the bully and I became friends. He came out to the farm a few more times and spent the night, and I stayed at his house a couple of times as well. Then I went away to boarding school and we lost touch for a while.

Some years later at a local football game, three thugs from another town saw me coming in and were trying to get smart and start a fight. My old friend, the bully, just happened to come up, saw what was happening, and said, "You'd better leave him alone or you're gonna be dealing with me." They all dropped their heads and said nothing.

His reputation had preceded him and that was the end of that. Everybody knew him and most stayed clear of him. It was said he eventually got into it with the toughest, meanest, and most troublesome man from around this area. They had an epic fight, and the man was so badly beaten he left town. Some people considered my bully a hero after that.

Looking back on those years growing up at Claiborne, I was no angel. I was always getting into something—or sometimes getting out of it. My very first memory is trying to figure out how I could get out of my playpen. And not long after that, I remember playing in a sand pile in the backyard, which had a little picket fence around it where I played with toy trucks and tractors and shovels. Once, when the nanny wasn't watching, I dug a hole under the fence and slipped away looking for something else to do, which caused a household panic.

And I was always pulling pranks to surprise or scare people. I must have gotten this from my mother who enjoyed things like that.

I remember hiding behind or perching above doors so I could spring out like a panther trying to scare my sister, Clay. I once took my little sister, Dell, who is ten years younger, to the back of the farm to "explore the magic land" because I knew she would hear the fearsome rumbling of the four o'clock choo-choo train. The tracks came right by the farm, but you couldn't see them through the woods from back there. When I heard the train coming, I said, "What's that? Something is coming for us." The poor little thing was terrified.

I did a lot of things like that to my brother Seth. One Thanksgiving, long after we became adults, he reminded me of the day I was sixteen and he was about nine when I talked him into standing behind a large cedar tree and warned him not to peek out while I shot at it with a shotgun. We walked down and looked at the tree and you could still see the marks of the buckshot. We both laughed.

Another time, I took him down to the cow barn where there was always straw piled up beneath the loft door and I said, "We're going to jump into this." He was afraid to jump, and I told him, "If you don't, I'm going to push you."

He jumped and thought it was fun. Then, as he was about to jump a second time, I warned him to land in the exact same place because there was a pitchfork hidden in there. There wasn't really. I just wanted to scare him. I still remember the expression on Seth's face.

A few months later, we were flying a kite and it got caught on the end of a limb of a big tree in the yard. I said, "Seth, you're lighter than I am. You need to go out there and get that; it'll hold you, no problem. It'll be fine." So, he crawled out there and he got the kite. Then he got scared and wouldn't come back.

I said, "Come on back, or I'm gonna go down to the garage and I'm gonna get a saw and saw off that limb."

He wouldn't come back so I got the saw. He was out there frozen. I wasn't really going to saw it and make him fall. He was thirty feet up in the air. But I liked to imitate those villains I had seen in movies, and I pretended I was one, laughing and howling, climbing the tree with the saw. He started screaming bloody murder and Nathan, who heard the commotion from the house, came out and yelled at me, "What are you doing?"

"I'm gonna saw him down," I said.

Nathan ran back into the house and came back out with a twenty-gauge shotgun, which made him look bigger than he was. We both knew it was always unloaded, but he pointed it up there at me anyway, and said, "Drop that saw."

I said, "Nathan, I'm not going to— I'm just trying to scare him."

He said, "Drop that saw."

I dropped the saw and Nathan climbed up in the tree, got Seth's confidence, and they climbed down together. Nathan laughed and said, "You always gotta stir some shit."

One day when I was eight years old, my father told me it was hog-killing time and that he wanted me to get in the car and go with him to see a festive old Kentucky tradition. He said I needed to learn the realities of life and where all that good bacon that I had been eating came from.

We got in the car and went way back on the farm where this event took place each year. I remember driving up and seeing a small crowd of men gathered around a pen where there were four hogs. There was also a big steaming tub of very hot water and a tractor with a chain on the lift in front from which they hoisted the hog into the scalding water once he had been shot and killed.

We got there about the time Tee Osborne had picked up the .22-caliber rifle with which they dispatched the hogs. As a young farm boy, I was a pretty good shot with a BB gun, and my father thought it would be a good idea for me to shoot one of the hogs so I could really understand what making a living farming was all about.

I remember thinking that I didn't want to kill one of those hogs, but all of the men thought it would be a good idea for "Little Arthur" to "git one of 'em." They gave me the rifle, and my father said, "When that big fat one right over there comes around here close, shoot him right behind the ear." I remember the pig playfully looking right at me as I pulled the trigger. He let out a nightmarish squeal and hit the ground in contortions. Apparently, my shot was not quite on the mark. Tee took the gun and put it on the hog's head and finished him off.

The men all said, "Little Arthur, you done a fine job. You gonna have bacon, ham, and sausage for Christmas."

Killing that hog was something that haunted me for a long time and sometimes during the dead of night when I was lying in bed, I could hear him squealing.

Hog-killing time at Claiborne came to an end sometime during the sixties. Each year at Christmas time, my father would give each employee a hog as a bonus. One particular year, the IRS was auditing Claiborne and one of the agents told my father that the hogs would all have to be taxed and that he could not freely give them to the employees.

This made my father absolutely furious, and I remember him flying into a rage about it. When the agent came back in the spring to continue with his magnifying-glass audit of the Claiborne finances, I happened to be in the office one day when he asked my father, "Now, what about those hogs, Mr. Hancock?"

My father said, "They all died."

"Arthur had a little lamb, its fleece was white as snow. And everywhere that Arthur went, the lamb was sure to go." That's the way it was. I named him Lambkin.

A couple of years after I went to the hog killing, the Claiborne farm manager Harris Robertson gave me a little orphan lamb only a few weeks old. My parents said that I could have him and raise him. My father said this would be my first hands-on experience with livestock. Little did I know what he meant by that.

We were virtually inseparable. I fed Lambkin with a bottle for a long time, and he loved me. To him, I was his mother. To me, he was like a dog: my buddy, my pal, and my friend. He would follow me all around the yard, and I was able to keep him in my room until he grew larger. Then I kept him outside on the porch.

He was a character and would play around and buck with a gleam in his eye. He was about 150 pounds when he got into my mother's flowerbed and damaged some of her most cherished flowers. When my mother discovered their destruction, Lambkin just happened to be standing right in the middle of them, and as she was stooping down to salvage what she could, Lambkin came up behind her and butted her, pitching her forward into the flowers.

That night at supper I was told that I needed to sell Lambkin because he was getting too big and out of hand. I was very upset. I was going to have to sell my best friend. Daddy said it would be a good experience, and that he would bring around twenty dollars. Back then, you could go to the picture show and buy popcorn and a Coke for about a dollar, so twenty dollars sounded like a fortune. It was big money to a young boy.

A couple of days later, my father took me and Lambkin to the Paris stockyards. On the drive into Paris, I told Daddy I didn't want to sell him, and couldn't we just give him away to someone? He just kept talking about the twenty dollars and all that I could do with it, which took my mind off of the real issue.

When we got to the stockyards, I was sort of stunned and taken aback by everything that was happening. Right away, a big red-faced man met us, shook hands with my father and me, and told me to bring Lambkin on over to a scale that was nearby. I was getting up the nerve to strongly protest the whole thing, because in a naive way, I had thought I could talk my father out of selling him at the last minute.

Then, everything happened so fast. The man whose name was Red Florence took Lambkin off the scale and in an instant pushed him over into a pen with about a hundred other lambs. I ran over to try to get him, but I couldn't pick him out of the crowd. I called and called out to him. But then someone opened a gate, and they all went down a long line toward a larger pen filled with other lambs. Nothing could be done. I started to cry but didn't want these big men to think I was a sissy. And about that time Red Florence came up to me and gave me $18.50. For many nights I cried myself to sleep about what I had done to my dear Lambkin.

On a lovely fall evening in 1957, when I was fourteen, the entire family was up at the pool at Claiborne House getting together to have dinner when I brought up something that I had read in the *Lexington Herald* that morning about how the Russian spaceship Sputnik had attained speeds of well over fifteen thousand miles per hour.

As soon as I said this, my father told me that it did not go 15,000 mph, it went 10,000 mph.

I said, "Daddy, I read in the paper this morning that it goes over fifteen thousand miles an hour."

He said, "Don't contradict your father," and I said, "Daddy, I don't mean to contradict you, sir, but I swear to God, I read it in the paper this morning, and I'll be glad to go get it and show you exactly what it says."

"Goddamn it, Arthur," he said, louder this time, "*Don't contradict your father!*"

Perhaps it was my personality trait of always wanting to stir things up, but I followed close behind pursuing my cause when he walked away, balancing a tray of large steaks. My mother, sister, and brother were nearby, watching us as he laid the large sirloins on the grill.

I just couldn't help myself and brought up the subject again. "Daddy, I know you are a man who always believes in the truth and telling it like it is, so I am wondering and asking if we couldn't just go over the facts again about the Sputnik air speed."

"You don't know any more about outer space than you do about anything else," he said. "I could care less how fast the damn thing goes and that's the last word I ever want to hear about it."

I was standing behind his back, and, in a mocking way, I looked over at my brother and sister and smiled, and for their benefit, shook my fist at him.

My father had hands bigger and thicker than those steaks, and I never saw coming the one that landed on my jaw with such force it sent me flying over the top of a row of bushes. I saw my brother Seth running toward the house and heard my sister Clay crying, "Oh lord, Daddy's going to kill Arthur." Mama was somewhat amused by the drama.

I was lying flat on my back when Daddy walked up, stood over me pointing his finger and said, "Never double up your fist behind a man's back, Bud."

I had no idea he would see me, but we had been facing away from the setting sun and it cast a shadow of me and my raised fist on the ground right in front of him.

With my family in the early 1960s, Seth and Dell, Daddy and Mama and my sister Clay
— Hancock Family Photo

PART
TWO

CHAPTER 3

Little Enis and the Canary

WHEN I WAS SEVEN years old, I was watching a show on television called the *Louisiana Hayride*. Hank Williams stepped up to the microphone and came on singing and playing a guitar. It just fascinated me. Then I saw a real guitar propped up in the corner of Mr. Harold Johnson's house and knew instantly I wanted to play one.

I ended up getting a ukulele first. Then my mother bought me an eleven-dollar Stella guitar from Sears & Roebuck and my first cousin, Chilly Cox, showed me some chords and taught me to play. A song called *Mexican Joe* was the first one I ever learned to sing.

"Dancin', romancin', always on the go . . .
Sun shinin' down. . .
On Mexican Joe . . ."
—MITCHELL TOROK

With my first guitar, a Stella, a gift from Mama when I was 11. Practicing in my cabin at Lookout Mountain Camp in Mentone, Alabama, 1954 – Hancock Family Photo

The "toolshed" was a barn on Claiborne where they kept farm parts and feed for the horses. One rainy afternoon, when I was about ten, I went there and was in the loft looking through some of the old stuff they had brought to Claiborne from Ellerslie, the old Hancock farm in Virginia. I came across a very old Victrola with several records sitting nearby. I had never seen anything like it because there was a crank that you had to turn, which would make the record play.

I cleared away the dust and put on an old 78-rpm record and began turning the crank. I never heard such sounds in my life. The record was one of the first ever done by the Carter Family and every song on it was absolutely beautiful and extremely moving. I sat in that barn all afternoon and cranked and cranked and played that record over and over. That was one of my first forays into the fascinating world of bluegrass music.

I felt the same way when I was a little younger. During the summers in Nashville, my grandmother would take me to the Grand Ole Opry. We had great seats in the second row. I saw Hank Williams perform in person no more than twenty feet in front of me, and I got goose bumps when I heard the announcer say, "And from the great state of Kentucky, here's Bill Monroe and his Bluegrass Boys." They rapidly walked out on the stage and the banjo, mandolin, guitar, and fiddle went into overdrive. I was thrilled, fascinated, and hooked!

When I was a seventh grader at the Paris City School, a couple of friends and I went down behind the school to watch the band practice. We had been invited by Mr. Swickley, the band leader, whose invitation permitted us to have the best seat in the house. We sat right up close to the band members while they were ardently rehearsing for the coming football game on Saturday.

I can still remember the majorettes with their twirling batons, and the band members decked out in all of their magnificent colors, marching to the inspiring music and the thunderous beating of the drums. But I was especially fascinated with the trumpet section, their precision, and how they walked in perfect formation, swaying in unison from side to side.

All afternoon I dreamed about getting a trumpet and playing in the band. This is what I wanted to do, and I thought I could do it well. So that night at supper with Mom, Dad, and Clay, I said,

"Daddy, would you buy me a trumpet, please, sir. I really want to play in the band."

You would have thought someone had hit my father in the back, because he suddenly threw down his napkin, stiffened up in the chair, and glared at me. He said, "Well, I'll be a sonofabitch. When we were at Princeton, we all wondered who would have the goddamn son who wanted to play in the band, and I've got him."

That ended my aspirations of ever being in the band or playing the trumpet. I felt crushed and insignificant. *Why am I that bad, what's wrong with me?*

It set off a spark of resentment.

I was only thirteen when I was invited to perform on a popular country radio station out of Lexington, WLAP, The Mickey Stewart Show. The Claiborne farm manager, Harris Robertson, drove me to the station where I sang two songs, *Why Baby Why* and *Hey Joe.*

Several calls came into the show saying how much they enjoyed it, and someone called from the farm and said all the people working at Claiborne loved it and were very proud of me. Everyone who knew me was listening and I felt like a little hero. I was a star-struck teenager.

Mr. Harris brought me back to Claiborne House, and we got there just in time for lunch. I got out of the car and happily thanked him, and carrying my guitar, excitedly walked in the house and into the family room where my father was sitting and reading the *Daily Racing Form.*

I appeared at the door and my mother stood up and said in her beautiful southern accent, "Oh, Ahhthuh, you wuhh simply magnificent."

Daddy looked up from his paper and in his low voice calmly said, "Well, I'll be goddamned, if it isn't the canary come home to roost."

Penned by my friend William Hamilton – The New Yorker

In 1955, Grand Ole Opry star Porter Wagoner had a hit song called *A Satisfied Mind* that went like this:

> *"How many times have you heard someone say,*
> *if I had his money, I could do things my way . . .*
> *But little they know that it's so hard to find . . .*
> *One rich man in ten with a satisfied mind."*

One day, I was playing that song for my mother with my father in a room nearby within hearing distance.

When I got to those lines, I sang them louder because I really wanted him to hear it. There were many times back then when I wished that I had been poor. That song expressed my philosophy perfectly at the time. I went through a stage where I really didn't want to be a Hancock and be different from my friends in Paris. I'm one hundred percent sure I'd have gone into music had I been born with nothing.

Daddy heard the lines, came walking into the room and said, "That song is based on a fairy tale. One poor man in a hundred has a satisfied mind."

His message was that I would be among the dissatisfied poor if I continued to pursue music—and that he disapproved of Mama's obvious encouragement in that direction.

Mama once told me, "Ahhthuh, sometimes I think yo daddy is jealous of you."

Whatever was on his mind, it had become perfectly clear that what had come between Daddy and me was a serious and perhaps permanent conflict of interests. He hated the guitar. The whole idea of it was in direct conflict with his idea of what I was to do with my life.

About four o'clock one afternoon, when I was in my room with my new Martin guitar that my grandmother gave me, he knocked on my door and stuck his head in and asked if I wanted to go through some mares and foals with him. I was working hard figuring out the guitar riff on Del Shannon's song, *Runaway* and had been making progress. So, I said, "Daddy, I've been working on this song, and I've almost got it down. I would love to go another time, so please give me a rain check."

"Well, you are just like a goddamn parrot. If you knew half as much about pedigrees as you do those damn songs, you might amount to something in this business," he said. "You know what you remind me of?"

I said, "No, sir."

"The goddamned court jester."

I never heard a door slam louder.

With Henry Gregory entertaining at the Woodberry Forest Mid-Winter Dance in Orange, Virginia, 1959
– Hancock Family Photo

When I was fourteen, a couple of older friends came by and picked me up and we all went to Joyland Park in Lexington where the local musical hero and his band were playing in the ballroom. His name was Little Enis and his band was called the Table Toppers. Enis was very talented and sang great rock 'n' roll as well as country.

One of the boys that I was with knew him, and when Enis took a break, went up and told him about me and asked if I could get up and sing. Enis told him to go get me and I could open the next set.

When I met him, Enis and I immediately hit it off and liked one another. He told me, "Git up here, boy, and show 'em what you got."

I sang two songs, *Poor Little Fool* by Ricky Nelson, and *Party Doll* by Buddy Knox. The crowd loved it. Enis was smiling, the band really liked what I had done, and I got off the stage feeling like I was on cloud nine and that I was really accepted and appreciated.

Word got around Claiborne about my performance, and someone told my dad about "Little Arthur" knocking them dead at Joyland Park playing with Little Enis and the Table Toppers. A few days later at lunch, my father glared at me and said, "Who in the hell is some sumbitch named Little Enis."

I tried to tell him that Enis was a great guy and a great singer, but he just laughed and said, "Why in the hell would a man want to call himself Little Enis?"

I had no answer for that except to say that his real name was Carlos Toadvine. But it upset me because I really respected and appreciated Enis for his talent and for letting me play with him and his band. I made up my mind right then that I was going to keep playing music and if Daddy didn't like it, then so be it.

Maybe Daddy was the way he was to me because that's what it took for me to learn a dose of the tough love like that described in a Johnny Cash hit song entitled *A Boy Named Sue*:

> *"Son, this world is rough and if a man's gonna make it,*
> *he's gotta be tough."*

Daddy was just following through on his often-repeated axiom. "Be a man, Bud."

When I first began to drive a car, my father told me to always be home by eleven o'clock sharp. That worked out very well all summer until about ten o'clock one night when I went to Roselawn's drive-in to get a cheeseburger and a Coke.

I thought I had plenty of time, but they were fairly busy that night and at ten fifty I still hadn't been served. I asked the waitress, and she said it would only be a few minutes, so I went over and borrowed the phone and called home to tell my father that the order was almost ready and that I would be right there as soon as I could. He didn't say a word and I could hear him hanging up the phone.

I ate the cheeseburger and drank the Coke as quickly as I could. I hurried back to Claiborne House and parked in front of the four large columns. I went up the wide stone steps and quietly opened the front door. Just as I turned around to close it, my father stepped out from behind the shadows and hit me so hard it knocked me into a corner.

He said, "Goddamn you. I told you to be in at eleven o'clock!"

I jumped up and said, "Daddy, I am so sorry but, as I told you, it took them forever to bring the cheeseburger and the Coke and I didn't want to run out of there without getting my order."

He was enraged. No sooner had I gotten the words out of my mouth than he hit me again with his huge right hand. That blow knocked me over onto the steps that led upstairs. This time I didn't get up.

Then he told me to get down to my room. I lived in the basement. I got up and started down the hallway and he kicked at me and yelled at me to get the hell on downstairs. I began to run, with him right behind me still trying to kick me like he had done with the steak thief, Mike.

I beat him down the stairs and ran into my room and sat trembling on my bed. He came in and stood over me with his right fist drawn and said, "By God, when you drive my car, live in my house, eat my food, and sleep in my bed, you follow my orders. When I tell you to be in by eleven o'clock that means eleven o'clock. You've got a lot to live up to and you better damn well get some discipline. You can't be out there running around with all those hoodlums in Paris. Do you understand me?"

"Do you understand me?" he repeated.

I said, "I understand."

A half-century later and looking back, it all appears quite different. He was already mad at me for a stunt I had pulled only a week or so before. Late at night and without his knowledge, I had taken his new Oldsmobile for a joyride with a friend and two girls from Paris, which he only learned about because we were seen driving around the town square. Surprisingly, his only punishment had been a lecture and a lesson that I could have been arrested for car theft.

But that night, I can still remember sitting there shaking violently and looking up at those cold, light blue steely eyes. I decided then and there that if he hit me again, I was going to spring on him like a panther. I had taken all I could take.

CHAPTER 4

Nashville

IN MY LAST YEAR at the prestigious Woodberry Forest School in Virginia, I ranked in the lower half of sixty-four classmates, with the dubious honor of having received the most demerits of any student in the history of the school. One month I ranked eighth in the class, but the next month I was sixty-fourth, having become more interested in being a "River Rat on the Rapidan" and playing the guitar than studying. Nobody could believe that Vanderbilt University had accepted me as a student in the 1961 freshman class for the fall semester in view of my record.

Everyone in my astonished family celebrated my Vanderbilt letter of acceptance, especially my mother's family in Nashville where the name of her late father, Seth Walker, who had died a decade earlier, was still spoken with awe and reverence.

Then a second letter came from the Vanderbilt admission office like a punch in the gut. I had not been admitted after all. A letter announcing the acceptance of another "Arthur Hancock" had mistakenly been sent to me. We were all devastated.

Aunt Katie and her husband, Uncle David Keeble, a lawyer who worked in my grandfather's firm, soaked up the family disappointment and delivered it to the university officials. He told them that it wasn't fair to accept and then reject me and that I had already turned down admittance from other colleges. After being exposed to the kind of legal persuasion from Uncle David that had made my grandfather Seth Walker famous, Vanderbilt gave me another chance at admission: an IQ test that both Vanderbilt and my family hoped I would do well on but expected that I would not.

I don't remember the questions on the test, but they couldn't have been too difficult because I passed and was registered for the fall semester. I pledged to the SAE fraternity, which was important because that year there was a fraternity swimming competition. Being tall and lithe at six foot four and 182 pounds, I won—despite my handicap of still carrying a full head of heavy Elvis hair.

The university swimming coach, who was among the judges of the fraternity competition, saw potential and invited me to try out for the freshman swimming team. Not long after that, I accepted and got a buzz haircut.

Swimming became my most important achievement during my four years at Vanderbilt, although I did make an A in logic and a handful of other courses.

Some of my swimming records both at Vandy and other colleges were not broken for years afterward. In fact, I might never have graduated if I had not won the Southeastern Conference freshman class championship and followed that up my sophomore year by winning the Southeastern Conference in the hundred-yard freestyle.

History was the subject I enjoyed most and the one my Bachelor of Arts degree documented that I had studied. But the truth is that learning history, or any other subject, was not high on my list of interests. At Vanderbilt, my priorities were swimming, music, and having a good time.

NASHVILLE ON MY MIND

I'm headed down this highway, happy tears are in both eyes
Thinking 'bout my folks and friends and the sunny southern skies
This feeling's about the best I ever had and Lord I'm flyin'
Headin' south with Nashville on my mind

I'm leaving all the soot and smoke for fine and fresher air
To the only place in the U.S.A. there's music everywhere
Through the bluegrass of Kentucky across the old state line
Headin' south with Nashville on my mind

All the happiness I've known is waiting for me then
It's great to be in Tennessee and I'll soon be home again
The world of work and worry, all my cares I left behind
Headin' south with Nashville on my mind

The yes sirs and the no ma'ams and the kind and gentle tone
The operator's even nice when I'm on the phone
A better place on God's green earth I never hope to find
Headin' south with Nashville on my mind

All the happiness I've known is waiting for me then
It's great to be in Tennessee and I'll soon be home again
The world of work and worry, all my cares I left behind
Headin' south with Nashville on my mind
Headin' south with Nashville on my mind

The summer before I went to Vandy an Irish friend of my father, Lord Harrington, asked Daddy if his son could have a job working with the horses at Claiborne. At the time, he had the title of Viscount Petersham, but we all just called him Pete.

I had heard that the Irish were scrappers, and the viscount was quick to verify that. Our first outing was a dance in Lexington. Some guy kept following Pete around the dance floor and tapping him on the shoulder. Unfamiliar with the American tradition of breaking your dance partner, when the guy tapped for the third time, the viscount decked him.

With my great friend Pete Petersham at his father's home in Limerick, Ireland – Hancock Family Photo

One Saturday after work, we decided to go to Nashville because a friend of mine, Neil Cargile, had a large boat on the Cumberland River and was having a cruising party that weekend.

The party went on all day Sunday and about nine o'clock that night I said we needed to get on the road so we could be at work the next morning. But Pete had met a girl he really liked and told me not to worry. He said he would drive. Then he pulled out a sizable pill, which he said was a "Dexedrine Deluxe," that would keep him awake for the journey back to Paris.

We left Nashville around midnight, and I immediately went to sleep in the back seat. Pete was a very good driver who loved speed—and the new car my parents had given me as a reward for lasting five grueling years at Woodberry. It was a white Bonneville Pontiac convertible. About an hour had passed when I woke up on the other side of the car with my feet over my head after he had taken a curve too fast. I told him to slow the damned thing down.

The next time I awoke, it was to the sound of sirens and Pete saying, "Shall we have a go . . . shall we have a go?"

I said, "They'll shoot you over here, Pete. Stop the damned car!"

He pulled over and a state trooper came up and told the viscount that he had been called by the sheriff of Cave City, Kentucky, who had clocked him going through town at 100 miles an hour. The trooper said, "The sheriff will be here in a minute, so stay put."

The big-bellied, red-faced sheriff came up to the car a few minutes later and told the viscount he was going to jail. Pete politely told him he didn't realize that he was going so fast and that where he was from there was no speed limit.

The sheriff asked him where he was from and when Pete told him Ireland, the sheriff said, "Aww hail, thas whur my people's from." He asked for his driver's license which was the old international version that unfolded downward into four sections.

The sheriff said, "Whutt in the hail's this thang?"

Pete was a charmer, and it wasn't long before he and the sheriff were talking about Ireland and the names their families had in common.

I couldn't believe it when the sheriff said, "I ain't never met nobody from Ireland and for the sake of our kinfolks, I'm gonna let you go."

Then I opened my big mouth and made another of my many mistakes involving alcohol. Before we left Nashville, I had bought two fifths of Jack Daniels whiskey because it was so much cheaper down there. When the sheriff had arrived, he had taken them and put them in his cruiser.

As I was getting ready to sit down behind the steering wheel, I said something stupid to the sheriff, "Now can I have my whiskey back?"

He put his hand on his gun and told me, "Git in ye goddamned car and foller me down to jail."

I said, "Sir, I was just kidding. Go ahead and keep the whiskey." With that, he pulled his gun out, cocked it, and said, "I done told you once't, git in ye goddamn car and foller me down to jail . . . rat now!"

Pete and I spent the night in the Cave City jail, in a little town about halfway between Nashville and Lexington. Still half drunk, I slept while the viscount paced the floor all night long because he had taken the Dexedrine. The next morning, they brought us some cold eggs and a glass of water. The viscount took his eggs and threw them through the bars of a window to the tune of a robin singing outside. She never missed a note.

About nine thirty they took us before the judge. I told the viscount I was going to tell him the sheriff had stolen my whiskey. He erupted, "Mate, keep your fucking mouth shut. I will buy you two fifths of Jack Daniels when we get to Paris."

I did. The judge charged the viscount with reckless driving, speed-ing, and operating without a valid driver's license. Even though his international license was good in America, the viscount didn't argue. I was charged with permitting an unlawful driver to operate a motor vehicle. The sheriff stood nearby with a piggish and satisfied grin on his face.

The fine was $250, a sum so huge back then I had to call the bookkeeper at Claiborne and have the money wired down.

The Viscount Petersham eventually would become the twelfth Earl of Harrington, and it would be twenty-eight years before I took my last drink of alcohol.

With my trusty 1961 Bonneville Pontiac convertible in front of Claiborne House — Hancock Family Photo

Shortly after I got to Vanderbilt, three SAE pledges and I went out one night to have a few beers. We were leaving the bar not far from the university when two big raw-boned guys walked past our car. One of them said something to my friend Damon as he was getting in my car and Damon called him a sonofabitch. Two bottles of Budweiser immediately smashed into my windshield, and they ran at us trying to open the doors.

I knew exactly what we were dealing with when I heard their accents. They were mountain men. The mountains of Eastern Kentucky, North Carolina, and Tennessee are part of Appalachia where the people are cut from a different cloth. They are family-oriented, religious folks, but you cross them at your own peril. They speak the English language with a distinct dialect common to their region.

That night in Nashville, as the beer bottles hit the car, I knew we were in big trouble and took off. I looked in the mirror and saw them getting in their car to come after us.

I went flying down White Bridge Road to get away, but the three friends who were from Nashville kept saying, "Hancock, you damned Kentucky chickenshit, stop the fucking car."

I told them they didn't want any part of those guys. But my buddies kept saying there's four of us and two of them, and that if I didn't stop the car, I'd never live it down and I'd be known as a chickenshit all over campus. All this talk was of course fueled by the large amount of beer we had drunk, but I saw the writing on the wall and slammed on the brakes.

I opened the trunk and handed Damon the spare tire. He was a big football player. And I gave a hammer and a jack to the two other guys. I took the tire iron and put it in my belt behind my back.

We hadn't been stopped but a minute or so when their car came screeching up behind us and stopped about thirty yards away. They got out and started throwing empty beer bottles at us. Then, yelling and screaming obscenities, they charged us.

Damon threw down the tire and, as it bounced on the road, my buddies dropped the hammer and the jack and took off running full speed into the woods. Then the mountain boys came up to me and one split off to the right and the other to the left. "Putt che got damned knaf away," one of them said. I showed them the tire tool, dropped it, and said. "I don't have a knife."

Quick as a cat, the one on the left hit me right above the eye with a full bottle of beer and knocked me to my hands and knees. Then they took off into the woods after my friends. I remember one of them yelling, "Wur you at, you fat sonofabitch?"

I got back in the car behind the wheel and found a piece of cloth to stop the blood flowing from above my eye. Two or three minutes later, they came to the side of the car, and I expected the worst. Then one of them stuck out his hand and said, "Buddy, I wanna shake yore goddamned hand. You the only one of you sonofabitches ain't a chickenshit."

They got back in their car and took off. A few minutes later, the Vanderbilt men came out of the woods and told me that we never should have stopped. One asked me how I knew they were so rough.

"Because they are from up there in my neck of the woods and I know how they are."

I dropped my chickenshit friends off at their dormitory and drove over to the Vanderbilt hospital. The doctor came in where I was lying on a bed in the emergency room, and a nurse asked me what happened.

I was still mad and half high from the beer and the injury, so I replied, "Some mountain bastards hit me in the head with a beer bottle." The first thing the doctor said was, "Well, hail fahr! Now hold steel, buddy, whal I stitch yore head up." When I heard that accent, I kept my mouth shut, thanked him, and went back to the dorm with six stitches above my eye.

Back before the days of Wendy's, McDonald's, and interstates, I was driving through the Kentucky Mountains and stopped at a little restaurant. There was a counter with four seats and three tables in the back. I sat down in one of the seats and ordered a hamburger, french fries, and a Coke from a very beautiful girl behind the counter.

She had long black hair and lovely hazel blue eyes. I tried to carry on a conversation with her, but she seemed nervous and noncommittal, occasionally casting a glance at the bearded man at one of the tables, who kept staring at us.

I finished my lunch, paid the bill, and right before leaving, I said, "Give me your phone number and I will call you and come back down here and see you."

She said, "I don't have no phone."

I said, "Well, okay, that's fine, I'll just come back and see you here at the restaurant. I'll be back before long."

My car was parked right out front, and no sooner had I put the keys in the ignition and started the motor than the man with the beard appeared at my window. He reached in and grabbed me by the hair, jerked my head back over the seat, and stuck an eight-inch hawk-billed knife right against my throat.

His hands were trembling when he said, "Ahh don't wont to keel you, buddy, but ahh weel."

I said, "Sir, what did I do wrong?"

He said, "You bettuh git ye goddamned ass outa hure and don't you nevuh come back down hure no more."

I said, "Sir, I swear to God, I will never come back down here again, sir, never." He let go of my hair and kicked the car. My leg was shaking so badly that I had to push down on my knee to make my foot hit the accelerator. I scratched off and never went back. It was the last time I ever tried to pick up a mountain man's girlfriend.

The mountain men had earned my respect, and I wrote a song about them called *The Mountain Man*, which Grandpa Jones recorded.

THE MOUNTAIN MAN

Way down in ole Kentucky, Tennessee and Caroline
West Virginia and Virginia, to the Georgia Bama line
There lives a man unlike the men in the rest of this great land
He's a breed that's like no other, and he's called the mountain man

He's English, he's Scotch Irish, he's German and he's lean
And don't you make the sad mistake and think this man ain't mean
But where he lives he needs to be, it's a dark and bloody land
And life's no bowl of cherries for this backwoods mountain man

But the mountain man is a hell of a man, he don't beg or moan
Most of what he lives on, he's hunted or he's grown
He don't take no charity, handouts ain't his game
'Cause everything he's proud of is written in his name

You'll find him in the wildwoods or working on the farm
Layin' down an old oak tree to keep the family warm
Plowin' with a long-eared mule or trappin' in the creek
Or diggin' in a black coal mine for six long days a week

Hard times are his good buddies, and they treat him like a friend
No sooner than they've gone away they come right back again
But he just smiles and goes along and does all that he can
To let 'em know before they go, they can count on a mountain man

And the mountain man prays to the Lord to help him find his way
And guide him as he travels on until that final day
And he tries to do his best in life and never questions why
'Cause his mind is on the time he'll climb that mountain in the sky

Swim practice at
Vanderbilt
– Hancock Family
Photo

Co-Captain of the
Vanderbilt Swim Team
– Hancock Family
Photo

To become a competitive swimmer at Vanderbilt University, I had to quit drinking for four months every season. The team would meet at six in the morning and go over to the pool in the freezing cold. Then we'd train again in the afternoon from four to six. I was walking the straight and narrow.

But after I won the Southeastern Conference in 1963, we went out to party and I got drunk. I had been dating the same girl, Mamie, for some time and was sure we were in love. She was blonde and beautiful and loved country music. She was with me and there was a football player and his date in the back seat.

It was about ten o'clock at night and there was no traffic, and I was going a hundred miles per hour down West End Avenue not far from the university in my white convertible. I looked in the mirror and saw flashing lights. There were two cop cars after me. I hadn't even noticed.

We came to a stoplight, and one of them slid up beside me and one blocked me from the other way. The cops jerked me out of the car. I pulled loose from them. We had the radio going and I started doing the monkey all around the car. But not for long.

They threw me up on the car, handcuffed me, and took me to jail at the mammoth Davidson County Courthouse, which stands on the bluff of the Cumberland River like the crown on the head of a king.

Inside, on a lower floor, was a room with about five or six cops sitting around. I was real nice and apologetic and said, "I guess I messed up."

And they said, "Well, boy, we're gonna give you a breathalyzer test."

I didn't know what they were talking about. Then they brought out this wooden contraption with a glass bulb and a balloon on the end of it.

One of them said, "Now, you blow into here and we're gonna check to see how drunk you are and how much alcohol you got in your system."

I'd been training for months and months. I'd won the Southeastern Conference. I could swim 150 meters underwater and not come up for air. I could bench press over three hundred pounds. I was in superb shape.

He gave me the thing and said, "Now, take a deep breath and blow in it as hard as you can."

Maybe I didn't think I was going to blow it up, I don't know; but I do remember thinking, I'm gonna blow so hard into this damned thing, I'll break it.

So, I did. The balloon popped! The officers looked at one another and chuckled, wondering what to do next. They looked around but that was their one and only breathalyzer.

I said, "Well, I guess that's the end of that shit."

One of them said, "Boy, you think you're pretty smart, don't you?"

And I said something only a drunk would say. "Well, I am fairly smart; hell, I go to Vanderbilt." Then I said something even worse, "If all five of y'all came to Vanderbilt, put your minds together and took the art class, which is the easiest one there, you still couldn't pass the exam."

Right then, a little cop came up and grabbed me and put my arm behind my back and another one said, "Billy, put him in there with them fightin' drunks."

"Sir, I was just joking," I said. But they took me up these old, dank steps up to about the third floor. It stunk up there and I could hear all kinds of stuff going on. They marched me down a dimly lit hall and opened the door and it looked like a horror show in there. People had bandages on their heads and over their eyes and on their arms.

No sooner than he pushed me into that smelly cell, a big redheaded guy came up and said, "What you in here for, boy?"

I said, "I been doin' a little fightin'."

He was like the head dog in there, and I told him what had happened about blowing up the damn contraption and he and several others laughed.

There were about twenty-five people in the place and a bunch of bunks along the wall, so I went over to lie down on a bunk, and I heard somebody saying he was going to whip my ass. Then, the big redheaded guy said, "You touch that boy and it'll be the last person you ever touch."

He liked me, I guess, and I rolled over on the bunk and turned my back. Two or three fights broke out and then about an hour later they threw a black guy in there. He was out of his mind drunk, and all hell broke loose. This was about the time of Martin Luther King Jr. and the civil rights movement, and there was a lot of tension in the air. He started ranting and raving about black power, which didn't set well with the "fightin' drunks." They lit in on him and beat the hell out of him. I rolled over and saw that same little cop smiling and tiptoeing to watch it all through a window in the door.

I wanted to try and stop it but wouldn't dare do anything. I was in enough trouble myself. I remember feeling I'd be lucky to get out of that place alive. After three or four hours, Mamie came and bailed me out.

Succeeding in life meant everything to my father, and if there was ever anybody more competitive, I would like to meet him.

He was a very good amateur golfer and the Lexington Country Club champion in 1933. One year, he was playing in the amateur championship in Louisville when he got mad and threw his putter into the top of a massive oak tree where it lodged.

With no way to get it down, the caddy had to climb the huge tree and retrieve it for him. By the time he got down, Daddy, having somewhat regained his composure, told the boy that he was very sorry.

"Oh, don't feel too bad, Mr. Hancock," the caddy said. "There was some country sonofabitch down here two years ago who threw his putter all the way over the top of that same damn tree."

That "country sonofabitch" had been my father.

Daddy and some of his friends from Bourbon County had a regular golf date at the Stoner Creek Country Club in Paris. As the story goes, one day they had made some pretty hefty bets on the outcome. The sixth hole and green were located right next to Stoner Creek, which is about the size of a small river. The tee is about 150 yards from the green and the fairway borders the edge of the creek.

The game was close and the stakes high when my father took his shot. It clipped the limb of a tree along the creek and bounced out into the water. My father picked up his golf bag and slammed it on the ground. He had to hit the ball again, and his beautiful shot landed about three feet from the flag and left him with a score of three on a par three hole.

My father said that they should give him the damn shot because even a baby could make it. Of course, they made him take it because all the money was riding on every stroke. He putted the ball which went around and around the hole and then stalled right on the lip, so close that it could have dropped in at any second, but it did not.

Daddy exploded, took his golf bag and threw it out into Stoner Creek. Some of his friends howled with laughter, and his caddy made the grave mistake of joining them. Daddy grabbed the caddy, picked him up, and threw him out into the creek where the bag had landed. His feet were touching the bag on the creek bottom, so he went underwater, picked it out of the mud, and brought it back to my father, who was very embarrassed. He gave the caddy a fifty-dollar bill, and said, "Son, I am so sorry, and I apologize."

In the middle of the Great Depression, fifty dollars was a handsome reward. The other caddies looked at the fifty-dollar bill, grinning from ear to ear and all agreed when one said, "I wish the hell he'd a throwed me in thar."

My Daddy just could not bear to lose. I recall one night when he and Clay were happily playing gin rummy by the fire. Everything was nice and peaceful, and we all had a drink of Jack Daniels and water. I wasn't paying much attention to the card game and was chatting with my mother, when suddenly I heard my father say, "Sonofabitch, I can't win at anything!"

His voice was literally breaking with emotion. He stood up and grabbed the cards out of my sister's dealing hand, and the rest of the cards on the table, and then tried with his huge hands to tear the deck in half, but he couldn't do it. Failing at that, he violently threw them into the fire. Then he stormed out of the room and did not return for about fifteen minutes. Mama couldn't stop laughing.

Another time, when he and I were playing a game of ping-pong, I was ahead twenty-one to twenty, and had just hit a shot toward the left side of the table because he had gotten way over to the right side. When my shot was in the air and headed for the far corner of the table, he grabbed the table and pulled it out from under the ball. I said, "Daddy, how could you do that to me? I was going to win the game."

He told me he had to grab the table to keep himself from falling.

On the other hand, this incredible competitive spirit was supported by a work ethic second to none. He always said that if you're a busboy cleaning tables, clean every table to the very best of your ability and make it spic and span. Always do the best job you can in any task that you perform, and you will be just fine in life.

He never asked any less of me, even when I was a little kid.

Naturally, all of this was somewhere in the back of my mind the day in 1964 when he and Mama came to the University of Alabama my junior year to watch me compete in a big Southeastern Conference swimming meet. Having won an SEC championship as a sophomore, I was expected as the captain to lead the team to a win. But that day, I had to take on the Georgia Tech star swimmer, Larry Caghan.

I lost to him by a few fifths of a second. Afterward, Mama and Daddy took me out for dinner where I heard Daddy complain, "All I ever get are goddamned seconds!"

With friends, Chris Williams on keyboard, Bill Shwab, Mary Vance Noel, Mary Lynn Hartwell and Mamie Hutton in Nashville, 1962 — Hancock Family Photo

With "Nashville Cats" at Bill Shwab's family home – Hancock Family Photo

By the spring of 1965, I had gotten seriously behind in my work at Vanderbilt. My father once said that two years of college were all anyone ever needed to be in the horse business, and I had tucked that thought away in my mind. I went to see the dean and dropped out of school.

When I called my father and told him that I had dropped out of Vanderbilt and was ready to come back and go to work, there was about a five second pause and he said, "What in the hell do I need with a goddamn college dropout!"

Then he slammed the phone down and I was left sitting in the phone booth wondering what in the hell I was going to do now. He told the bookkeeper to cut off my allowance from the office and not to send me assistance of any kind.

I borrowed some money and flew to Chapel Hill, North Carolina to visit Bill Shwab, a lifelong friend from Nashville I had known from my summer visits to see my grandmother. Bill was then a student at the University of North Carolina. At one point while I was there, a friend of Bill's named George Butler and I went over to a Dr. Taylor's house to get some medicine for a cold.

When we got there, a lanky, sensitive-looking teenager was sitting on the porch smoothly stroking a guitar. I watched him, and he could really play. I was surprised at the sound of his licks and thought maybe I should just hang it up. Years later, and once he became a star, I realized that the boy on the porch had been James Taylor.

Before I left Chapel Hill, I bought a motorcycle on credit and rode it back to Paris and up the drive to Claiborne House.

My mother was standing on the front porch talking to a friend of hers when up rolled a big motorcycle carrying a man wearing a black sweater and black helmet with a visor over the front. I gunned the motorcycle several times as my mother stood there wondering what in the world was going on.

I removed my helmet and she suddenly seemed very relieved that I was not a Hell's Angel. She welcomed me with a loving-mother smile, and said, "Ohhh . . . Ahhthuh!"

Then I went to see my father. To say he was not very glad to see me would be an understatement. He told me to go get a goddamn job.

I rode the motorcycle back to Nashville and got one selling pots and pans, which turned out to be a weekly competition against three other salesmen. We would report in each week, and it seemed I always sold more cookware than the other guys.

The third week when we made our reports, the boss said, "Ain't this somthun! Golden boy has done outsold evabody again. I guess that Vanduh-vilt education done made him bettah than all the rest of us."

I told him he could take his goddamn pots and pans and shove them up his ass, and if he didn't like it to step his fat ass outside and

I would show him what a Vanderbilt student could do. He didn't do a damn thing but drop his head and sit there. The other salesmen stealthily smiled because they weren't fond of him either.

Obviously, I now had to find another job and once again my uncle, David Keeble, helped me out. He took me straight to the governor of Tennessee, Frank Clement, to see what jobs he might have open working for the state. Governor Clement got on the phone and called the highway department, and they told him that there was a supervisory position open for the Memphis area and Governor Clement told me I could have that.

I thanked him profusely but by that time I had decided I was going to try to get back into school and graduate. I had seen what it was like not to have a college degree while looking for a job and I wasn't sure I would ever work at Claiborne again.

Politely, I told him that I didn't expect to be working long at the state and any menial job available would be much appreciated. I said that I didn't want to fill a position and cut another man out of it, so he called them back and they said they needed somebody on a surveying crew because they were just in the process of building I-40, the interstate highway from Nashville to Memphis. So I got a job with a sledgehammer and a shovel.

After a couple of months of that, I wrote a letter to the dean at Vanderbilt and humbly told him how sorry I was I had left, and that it was the biggest mistake I had ever made in my life. I asked him to please consider letting me back in so that I could graduate. He took pity on me and said that because of my contributions to Vanderbilt swimming and the fact that I had been a model citizen, as far as he knew, he would grant me readmission. I graduated in January 1966.

Around the Vanderbilt campus in those days, the place to eat, drink, and be merry was called Ireland's. It was more of a Southern student hangout than Irish pub, its main attraction being delicious steak-stuffed homemade biscuits.

I was a pretty good guitar player and singer, or so I thought, until I heard some guys playing at Ireland's one night in 1965. They were the Bluegrass Boys, moonlighting between Grand Ole Opry appearances, apparently without the approval of the band's founder, the legendary Bill Monroe.

I had never heard anything like it. The lead singer was Peter Rowan, who after two years as the guitar player and singer with Monroe, went on to become a musical legend. I was surprised to learn that he was not a southern boy at all, but a Yankee from Boston, Massachusetts. He told me he lived just up the street and asked me to stop by sometime, which I did one afternoon. Pete and I exchanged a lot of old-time bluegrass mountain tunes as well as a strange little cigarette that he offered me. I inhaled!

Peter Rowan was the ultimate artist and musician. He told me one day that he believed there were some people that just always have a tune running through their head. Well, I was one of them.

We went out a few times together to catch the Rolling Stones on their first US tour, and to see Ike and Tina Turner at a nightclub in what was then called the "Negro" section of Nashville. We were the only white people who came to see the Turners and we didn't stay long. Some guys came over and said we were not properly dressed for the event. We must have looked pretty bad. We didn't argue. A fight had broken out on the other side of the room. I also took Peter to a black church in rural Tennessee, and he was very moved by the soul of the singers.

Over the next five decades, Peter became universally regarded as a musical genius, as adept with the mandolin as with the guitar and who possessed a uniquely flexible voice capable of melding with any note on either instrument.

I took away from my time with him a whole new definition of the word "musician". A few years later, some of those amazing bluegrass guitar runs and vocal skills Pete taught me helped me obtain a recording contract with Monument Records.

My longtime friend and musical inspiration, Peter Rowan – Atsuko Yasuda Photo

CHAPTER 5

The Oracle of Wisdom

MY FATHER WAS FOND of the adage that when you see a turtle on a fence post, you know he didn't get up there by himself. My life is one episode after another of being lifted onto that fence post by a Good Samaritan: none more important than the man I called the "Oracle of Wisdom".

Like so many other country songs, my *What of Tomorrow* was written in deep despair by a young lover with a broken heart. A first love is often the most difficult to forget. As a songwriter, I have learned that the pain or joy of a particular moment can be the wellspring of creativity, but that one bad line or forced rhyme can ruin an otherwise good song—or even a relationship.

In the case of Mamie, she was the source of both my sorrow and my first big break in the music business. But how the song I wrote about her reached number thirty on the Country Billboard charts nationwide and number one in Minneapolis-St. Paul and Greenville, South Carolina, had less to do with the song itself than with the genius of one Fred Luther Foster, founder of Monument Records.

WHAT OF TOMORROW

In yesterday, your strange expressions,
Filled me with trembling inside.
And now today your shy confessions
Oh lord only knows how I've cried.
Yet they can't take away the joys of yesterday,
But what of tomorrow.
So many times we've spent together
Few have known times such as those.
They were so dear, but now you'd rather
Bring all of these good times to a close.
Yet they can't take away the joys of yesterday,
But what of tomorrow.
I never dreamed of our love ending,
But now we have drifted apart.
All of the time that he's been spending,
My Darling, has taken your heart.
Yesterdays I must forget,
There will be unknown tomorrows.
There may be regret,
But today there's only sorrow.
And what of tomorrow,
What of Tomorrow.

Nashville music legend Fred Foster, founder of Monument Records — Foster Family Photo

At age eighteen, Fred had come off a North Carolina cotton and sorghum farm with an IQ of 160, a keen ear for music, and a sharp eye for undeveloped talent. His only real work experience had been plowing behind a mule and bussing tables at Hot Shoppe. When he died in February of 2019 at age eighty-seven, *The New York Times* called him the "Nashville Champion of Talent".

Among the stars whose rocket careers he helped launch were Dolly Parton, Roy Orbison, and Kris Kristofferson—just to name a few. There is hardly a big name in country music and R&B in those years that did not at one time associate with Fred and benefit from connections with him and Monument Records, which he founded in 1958. Before that he was a talent scout for Mercury and had worked at RCA.

He was already a legend when I met him in 1967 through my Uncle David Keeble, who had recently represented him in a divorce. Uncle David knew I had been writing songs at Vanderbilt. He thought the world of Fred and offered to introduce us.

Monument had a big office and a studio on Music Row, but because it was so noisy, our meeting was set at Fred's office north of the city out in Hendersonville, where both Roy Orbison and Johnny Cash lived. Uncle David gave me a map on how to get there and said Fred would give me sixty minutes.

I was twenty-four. I called Fred who told me to come in the front door, turn left, and just take a seat on the couch. So, I did, sitting there with my guitar, nervous as hell when all of sudden somebody just appeared and there was Fred. He was part Cherokee, and I would later learn that he could walk through the woods, and you couldn't hear him. He was thirty-five and looked like Dr. Spock with a toupee.

We talked and he told some stories and said he would love to hear some of my songs. I played him *Lonely, Lonely Me* and a song called

Karen. I was already nervous and had butterflies in my stomach when the star saxophonist Boots Randolph, the Kentucky Yakety Sax legend, came in and sat down with us.

I thought, well, that's it . . . I'm too nervous to sing. But then Fred asked me to sing my other song, *What of Tomorrow*. He really liked it and so did Boots.

Fred had a sixth sense for songs and published material others had passed over. He helped Willie Nelson get started and convinced Ray Price to quit singing like Hank Williams and get his own style, which made him a country star in a tuxedo. Fred always said that a star had his own unique voice—when you heard Johnny Cash, you knew it was Johnny Cash.

Fred signed me up that day. I didn't expect it. But he gave me a contract and said, "You're a good musician and that's a damn good song. You got the looks and you've got the talent. Let's give it a try."

He also signed me to his music publishing company Combine Music, to which he had just signed Kris Kristofferson. Next thing you know, Monument released three records and there was my picture in a big country music magazine as another up-and-comer discovered by Fred Foster.

In the fall of 1969, as a Monument artist, I was fulfilling my obligation to augment the nightly entertainment being offered in Boots Randolph's night club during the annual DJ convention held each year in connection with the Grand Ole Opry's birthday celebration.

The Carousel Room was a well-known bar in the world-famous Printer's Alley that showcased Boots, Chet Atkins, and the other "Nashville Sound" musicians who turned the town into Music City.

At the time, I had gone back to work at Claiborne and was still doing what Daddy had resented all those years—dividing my time and interest between his horse business and my music. He said you can't serve two masters, and you can only do one thing and do it well.

My arm was in a cast from an automobile accident in April of '69 that had nearly killed me. I couldn't play the guitar and I didn't have a hit record, so the best I could manage was to sing something that both the band and the disc jockeys knew. To be safe, I chose Hank Williams' *Your Cheatin' Heart*. It was not my favorite song and the disc jockeys, however important they might be to a new country singer, did not shape up as a good audience.

There was no danger they would give me bad reviews because not one of them was paying any attention to me. Through the dense curtain of smoke and loud talking, I caught a dim glimpse of a future I wasn't sure I wanted.

What I saw was a bunch of lounge lizards packed like sardines into a dingy cavern that needed pressure washing. Many of them were slugging down whisky, sucking cigarettes, and trying to work up something later with women who were not their wives.

The longer I sang, the clearer the picture became. Somewhere out there under the smoke and neon was a future in music I wasn't sure I wanted. The bluegrass of Kentucky was looking greener and greener.

I met Kris Kristofferson when he was sharpening pencils and sweeping up over at RCA. I had no idea he was a Rhodes Scholar and an Army captain who flew helicopters after completing Ranger school. He once rented a helicopter and landed it on Johnny Cash's lawn out on Old Hickory Lake just to pitch him *Sunday Morning Coming Down*.

With singer Ray Price, who recorded three of my songs – Hancock Family Photo

Kris Kristofferson, Fred Foster, Willie Nelson – Foster Family Photo

I was with Fred when he first heard the tape of Janis Joplin's recording of *Me and Bobby McGee.* Fred said, "My God, that's a smash hit." He was excited because he had given Kris the idea for the song, and Kris made him co-writer.

Another time, he played a tape Kris had sent him of *Loving Her Was Easier* and told me that Kris had written three new ones, and that one might make a good third record for me at Monument. Kris offered to come over and play them for us at the studio at the end of Music Row.

Kris came in with his guitar and I sat in the chair right across from him. He played *Darby's Castle, When I Loved Her,* and *Help Me Make It Through the Night.* When he was done, I asked him which one he liked the best. Kris was not only a great writer but a good salesman. He said he liked them all.

Fred was standing right behind me. I looked inquiringly up at him, and he said, "Arthur, I think I'd do *Help Me Make It Through the Night.*"

I said, "Fred. I don't need anybody to help me make it through the damn night. I think I'd like to do *When I Loved Her.*"

Well, here is "The Oracle of Wisdom", then the hottest record producer in Nashville, giving you his opinion. And if you don't have sense enough to follow his advice, he is not going to pressure or beg you to take it. He later jokingly told me he'd rather humor a fool as to argue with one.

That fall, Sammi Smith's recording of the song I turned down was the first big crossover hit in the history of Nashville music. It was called a watershed event for the industry: number one on the country charts and number eight on the pop. It sold two million copies, won a Grammy for Sammi Smith, all kinds of writing awards for Kris, and made them both famous.

Fred always told me he thought that if I had chosen music as a career, I would have been a success. And he told me more than once that *Help Me Make It Through the Night* could have had a similar impact on my career and changed the direction of my life forever. Destiny does indeed turn on a dime.

Although I knew by then not to question the judgment of "The Oracle of Wisdom," I knew myself even better than Fred did. And I know for certain today that if I had had a hit on *Help Me Make It Through the Night*, I probably would have ended up like Hank Williams or Keith Whitley. I would have been dead long ago.

When my friend and fellow songwriter, Marshall Chapman, introduced me to John Prine, I told him that story. He laughed and said, "*Help Me Make It Through the Night* don't need no help."

PART THREE

CHAPTER 6

Alcohol and Angels

I BELIEVE YOU are born with certain inclinations and interests. Mine was music. Bull Hancock had excelled in football and baseball at Woodberry and Princeton and had a boy who wanted to play in the band and was just the opposite of what he hoped his son would be.

Bull Hancock didn't like music, singers or dancers, or anything to do with that sort of thing. As a boy, when Mama got me a pair of tap shoes and I practiced on the concrete in the basement, he again suggested that I might be a sissy. When I was given a guitar by my grandmother on Mama's side, I was the "court jester," and when I sang Hank Williams songs on the local radio, I was the "canary".

He felt the same way about the way I looked. I had a lot of hair back then and many people were telling me how much I looked like Warren Beatty even though I was trying to look like Ricky Nelson, who was a big thing at the time.

My friends had nicknamed me *"Hawk,"* because when we went riding around Ft. Lauderdale looking for girls, I was usually the first to spot them. And around that time, I was even trying to get Daddy to buy me contact lenses so I wouldn't need glasses.

He said, "Goddamn you. All you think of is how you look. How do you think you're gonna make a living?"

My social life had become as irritating to him as my guitar. One day when I came home for lunch, he began cursing me and asking how I could "shame the family by screwing some girl in your little sister's bed."

My parents had returned home from a trip to find Claiborne House a bit disheveled and clear evidence of a party, including in my sister Dell's bedroom. I was the only one home and had no idea what he was talking about concerning Dell's room. But he kept asking about who all had been there over the weekend, and how could I have done such a thing. But it wasn't me.

He was so mad and so convinced I was responsible that he held it against me for days and was still so obviously pissed off at me that when we went to Churchill Downs a few days later to see one of our fillies run, his friend Warner Jones, who was at the time the chairman, called me aside and asked, "What's wrong with your father? What have you done now?"

Mr. Jones had introduced Daddy to my mother, and would later become a father figure to me, helping me with the same alcohol problem that he had. I told him I was innocent and knew nothing about how Dell's bed got messed up. At the time, Mr. Jones and I were walking a few steps behind Daddy on the way to the paddock, and he left me, caught up with my father, and put his arm around his shoulder. He said something I couldn't hear, and they both broke out laughing so hard that Daddy's neck turned red.

Mr. Jones later told me that he had reminded Daddy how once when they were young and my grandparents were gone on a trip that he and Daddy took some girls to the house and left the beds, the bathtub, and even the kitchen table in disarray.

It was not until sometime later when Seth came home from Sewanee that the mystery was solved. Seth had brought a bunch of his friends to Claiborne House for the weekend, and they had already gone back to school before my parents returned. Seth said it wasn't him either, but one of his friends.

To be honest, looking back, Daddy had many good reasons to consider me the usual suspect.

When I got home for Christmas vacation in my freshman year at Vandy, I went out with a couple of friends to Lexington to have a few beers. I got back to Claiborne House around midnight and was sitting in the library having a nightcap of Maker's Mark as I had seen people do in that room most of my life. I was two months shy of my nineteenth birthday.

Right away, a girl arrived who was spending the night with my sister Clay. Her date dropped her off at the front door and she walked into the library. She was a very pretty girl from a prominent Lexington family. She had obviously already been drinking.

She said, "How about a drink?"

"By all means," I replied.

I poured her a double bourbon and water, put on a Kingston Trio album and we sat down on the couch together. I remember lighting the fire and fixing us both another drink.

That is all I really remember until six o'clock the next morning when I woke up with a severe pain shooting from my left ear all the way down to my shoulder and arm.

My father had me by the ear and was pulling me right off the couch. I thought he was going to tear my ear off. I grabbed his arm to help relieve the pain and quickly got to my feet and saw the girl lying there on the couch with her dress up around her neck.

In a low menacing voice, he said, "Now get your ass down to your goddamn room, you common bastard. Dirtying our household . . . you goddamn dog."

I tried to take off running but my pants were around my ankles, and I tripped. About that time, he kicked me so hard in the ass that I fell forward flat on my face. I got to my feet but there was no use trying to run because my pants were tangled around my ankles. All I could do was take giant hops toward the hall and the steps that led down to my room in the basement.

Daddy was right behind me still trying to kick me, but I was in very good condition from being on the swimming team and was probably hopping eight or ten feet with every jump. When I reached the steps to the basement, I jumped from the top step to a platform about halfway down and leapt over the banister. Then I hopped in my room and shut the door.

Mama had found us and, not knowing what to do, had gotten my father to wake me with a vice grip to the ear. Apparently, the girl was so zonked she slept through it all and my mother later told me she was able to cover her with a blanket before she woke up.

I knew there was going to be hell to pay so I threw some things in a suitcase, went out a window from my room, got in my new Pontiac, and headed back to Vanderbilt. I didn't call home for a couple of weeks, and nobody called me.

One Sunday afternoon in late August, after I had been back on the farm that week helping cut tobacco with a crew that included two good-looking girls from the mountains, I had invited them to come up to the pool at Claiborne House to go swimming after work and had asked my friend Paul Sullivan to come join us. Mama and Daddy were in Saratoga and were not expected home till later that night.

When we all got in the pool, I took off my bathing suit and was paddling on my back, testing the water for what I hoped might happen later. I was saying, "Periscope up, periscope up" and listening to their laughter that suddenly ceased. When I looked up, it was obvious why.

A young Paul Sullivan – Sullivan Family Photo

There at the end of the pool stood my father with his hands on his hips. I took a deep breath and dove straight to the bottom of the deep end where I must have stayed for two minutes—hiding and putting my bathing suit back on. When I came up, everybody else was already out of the pool and I heard Daddy telling Paul, "Don't you ever come out here again if you can't act any better than this."

The girls had gone to the house and didn't hear him calling them "riffraff" and lecturing me to never bring "those kind" over again.

In those days, before Paul joined the Air Force, got a law degree, and distinguished himself as a very prominent attorney in Lexington, my father had disapproved of our friendship. He had something against Paul's grandfather—he was the stockyard man who handed me the check for Lambkin—and had complained to Mama that if my grandfather was still alive, he would have been livid at the thought of me hanging out with Red Florence's kin.

My parents had viewed some of my childhood friends as not being from our world and potentially bad influences. Daddy was always asking me why I didn't hang out with those nice young men who played golf at the Idle Hour Country Club in Lexington. And every time I introduced a new acquaintance to my mother, she asked, "Ahhthuh, what does his fathah do?"

When I was twenty-six, Betty Parrish, daughter of Daddy's close friend Mr. Doug Parrish, and my sister Clay's best friend, got married in a big formal wedding on their farm. The groom was a nice fellow named Jimmy Kenan who had invited some of his college pals from the Ivy League. As usual in those days, I had a lot to drink. Funny—weddings always affected me that way. The wedding couple had already departed, and I was standing in the tent in my tuxedo with a bourbon in my hand talking to the visiting groomsmen—a guy from Yale, a star fullback from Dartmouth, and a writer for *Newsweek*.

The Vietnam War was on everybody's mind. A second cousin of mine, Eddie Keeble, had died in a helicopter crash over there and one of my dearest friends, Bill Shwab, was a Marine who had been wounded twice and was still there somewhere in the jungle. We were all drinking and talking about the war when one of them began mouthing off about how America had no business over there mistreating the Vietnamese.

Maybe because the Parrish home looked like it might have been built during the Civil War, the fullback, who was from Philadelphia and looked like he weighed about two hundred and thirty pounds, started talking about how the South still mistreated black people. I said I had not been brought up that way.

After hearing my position on that subject, the magazine guy pointed to some of the help serving drinks on the other side of the wedding tent and suggested that one of them might make a "good date" for my sister, Clay, who was standing nearby. I had known the bartender since my childhood. This was 1969. Things were different back then. This magazine guy from somewhere up north was deliberately looking for an insult that would rile me. I was easily riled in those days, and he got his wish.

About that time, my friend Louis Haggin III, whose father helped found Keeneland, walked up and joined the circle.

I said, "Louis, do you have a cigarette on you?" Like I was introducing him. He said, "No, I don't." That was a diversion for my attack.

When I whirled around, the fullback was standing between me and the magazine guy, maybe incidentally, but to me it looked like a kind of stand guard position with his fists on his hips, glaring at me. So I hit him first, so hard that my feet came up off the ground. He went sailing on his back across the tent floor. Now the Yale guy was in my way, so I decked him, too, and started after the magazine guy who had taken off running.

Then Shack Parrish, Betty's cousin, came running up yelling, "Arthur, you're ruining Betty's wedding." And I unleashed on him with a right hook that knocked him into one of the long tables with the whiskey and seltzer bottles. That thing crumpled and went down with bottles flying everywhere.

I went berserk looking for the magazine guy, but Louis Haggin came up yelling, "Quit, Arthur," and grabbed me from behind, pinning my arms. He was a big, strong guy and I was trying to pull away when he called out to my pal Dave Parrish, Betty's brother, "Dave, you got to knock him out."

I remember hearing Dave saying, "I can't hit my friend," and Louis saying, "You better hit him before he gets us. I can't hold him much longer." So, all six foot six of Dave reared back, hit me, and knocked me out cold.

I woke up in a car with a guy named John Beam just as we pulled out of Mr. Doug's driveway. I said, "Beam, what are you doing?"

"Taking you home," he said.

I said, "Beam, I'm gonna kill you." And I was only half-kidding.

When I got home, Daddy was waiting in my room in the basement. Somebody had called him and told him what had happened. He told me to get my things and get out. I was trying to tell him what happened when Mama appeared at the door and said, "Bull, let him go to sleep and you all can talk about it in the morning."

Daddy looked at her and then unloaded on me. All I remember is that next morning there was blood all over and my watch was broken and lying up against the wall.

Daddy was sitting in his office when I got upstairs. He said, "Get your stuff and get out."

I said I was going but I wanted to tell him what happened first—all about Vietnam and what the guy said about my sister Clay. I told him the whole story.

"That's why I did it," I said, "And I would do it again. I'd do it right now."

He got up from his chair and walked around the room for a minute and then came over to the chair where I was sitting and said, "What do you think would happen to you if you worked for IBM?"

I said, "Well, I'm sure they would fire me, Daddy."

He said, "Well, you go up there and apologize to Mr. Doug and see what he says. I've got to think about this."

I called and Mr. Doug was waiting for me in the tent beside his house. He said with a kind of chuckle, "Arthur, you really pulled one last night, didn't you?"

He took me over to where I had hit the fullback, and there was a trail of blood from where he had landed and slid across the floor all the way to where he pulled himself up by using one of the tent poles. There was even blood going up the pole.

Mr. Doug said, "You must have laid one on him."

I told him exactly what happened, and he said, "I don't blame you. Those are nice boys, but damn, I guess that whiskey gets to talking. It's okay. Hell, more and more, you remind me of your daddy. He got in some of these kinds of things when he was young."

When I got back home, Mr. Doug must have already called Daddy because he said, "Bud, I've been thinking about this." Then, with a faraway look in his eyes, he said, "I was once like you. Now you get ahold of yourself and be at work tomorrow."

Wrecking the Parrish wedding was the beginning of a pattern of disruptive behavior involving alcohol that not only distressed my family and friends but came close to ruining my life altogether.

I was still working at Claiborne about a month after the wedding when I had a bad wreck on the Lexington Road around midnight and nearly killed myself.

After being out with friends in town, I fell asleep at the wheel driving home and hit an electric pole which caused all of the lights in north Lexington to go out. This actually saved my life, because a state trooper came looking to see what had happened. He found me hobbling near the crash site among several downed electric lines with thousands of volts of exposed electricity. He put me in his car and rushed me to the hospital.

After the state trooper got me to the emergency room, he went back to the crash site, saw Daddy there and said he wanted to have some blood drawn from me for an alcohol level test. Daddy told him there was all the blood he needed inside that car and to leave me the hell alone.

I knocked out four front teeth, shattered a bone around my eye and slit my face open. My left arm was just hanging, broken in two places with the bones sticking out. I had broken all the ribs on my right side and one went through and punctured my lung. My left eye was closed and the whole side of my face was swollen. I would never look like Warren Beatty again.

Only my family and my best friend Paul were permitted to visit me in the hospital. I remember him coming in my room and when he saw me and the critical shape I was in, he looked very concerned, like he was going to cry. He says he thought I would never get out of there alive. I remember him saying I really needed to take care of myself because I was in such bad shape and could take a turn for the worse at any time.

I could sense how worried he was. I said, "Paul, did you see that redheaded nurse that was in here when you came in?"

He meekly said, "Yes, Arthur, I saw her."

I said, "Sullivan, I'm gonna get her when I get out of here."

To this day, he's always said that when I mumbled those words, he knew I was going to make it.

When I got out of the hospital, my sister Clay took me to the junkyard to see the Oldsmobile station wagon I had been driving. You could hardly tell it was a car. The engine was in the front seat and the upholstery was covered in blood.

The guy there took one look at me and said, "You wasn't in that thing was you?" I nodded affirmatively, and he said, "Go on, boy. We don't want no ghosts around here."

About eight months later, at a roadhouse in Nashville frequented by horse people and golfers, the fullback walked up to me and identified himself. My arm was still in a cast from the wreck and not knowing what he had in mind, I thought it might be revenge.

When he stuck out his hand, I didn't respond at first. But he had an amiable look on his face, and we soon were apologizing to each other for what had happened. He ended up telling me, "I've never been hit that hard in my life."

Running into him was another one of those you-can't-make-it-up instances that appear coincidental, but are they really? They say the first thing you learn in the CIA is that there's no such thing as coincidence. But the CIA doesn't believe in fate. The fullback ended up becoming the CEO of Bloomberg leading 10,000 colleagues by example.

In the fall of 1969, I met someone who would become known in my life as "The Ambassador," a guy from Houston, Texas named John Adger, who has filled a big space in my life ever since. He was exactly the kind of friend my parents had always wanted me to have.

Adger was tall, strikingly handsome, courteous, and charismatic. His mother's family was well-known and respected among Southern aristocratic landowners from down around Maury County, Tennessee, just south of Nashville. She and Mama had actually been friends in their youth.

We knew right off that John Adger was "somebody" because he was up in Kentucky as the date of a New York model named Dana who was staying at the home of Kenneth Franzheim II, a Texas multimillionaire who was ambassador to New Zealand at the time.

I ran into John at the same big Xalapa Farm training track where my sister Clay's bulldog Mike had destroyed the interior of Daddy's Oldsmobile. John told me that while he was in town, he had plans to talk to Daddy about breeding a mare he owned to Buckpasser, who was then a hot sire. I invited him over to Claiborne where he met my father, who liked him immediately, and gave him a contract for his mare Fast Cookie, who was co-owned by our neighbor Albert Clay.

With the mare Fast Cookie and her 1971 Buckpasser colt, The Scotsman, who ran 35 times and would become the first stakes winner raised by Stone Farm – Hancock Family Photo

Afterward, he was headed back to Nashville to visit his relatives and since I was going down there, I gave him a ride. Along the way, he invited me to go duck hunting in Louisiana that December.

I flew to Houston, and he met me at the airport. On the drive over to Louisiana, I saw a billboard with the face of a handsome young guy on it. I did a double take and it hit me. It was Adger, advertising some real estate business.

He and I have always laughed about me having only one good arm and trying to shoot ducks with the shotgun balanced on my cast, with him having to do all the work paddling the boat and wading it to and from the duck blind in the bayou mud.

We have been close friends for over fifty years. But he cannot claim that he had an immediate impact on my wild behavior.

With my friend John Adger duck hunting in Louisiana – Hancock Family Photo

CHAPTER 7

Wild Oats

BETWEEN THE AGES OF twenty-seven and thirty-four, I was working hard to become the professional horseman my father had wanted me to be. But I was also playing hard. As my father used to say, "All work and no play makes Jack a dull boy."

Susan, the daughter of the great trainer Vincent O'Brien, was getting married in Ireland. The O'Briens were longtime friends of my parents, and they invited me over to the wedding. Susan was marrying horseman John Magnier, who would later found Coolmore Stud and build it into the single most powerful breeding and racing operation in the world. Before I left, my mother made me promise that I wouldn't cause any trouble. She had good reason to be worried after what had happened at Betty's wedding. But neither one of us knew I was about to meet the "Princess of Prussia".

The Irish wedding was beautiful with wonderful music and lots of good food. I was on my best behavior, talking to people and having a great time, when I met a lovely girl and asked her to dance. She had deep-set blue eyes and long hair the color of honey. Her name was Renata. She was German and titled, the "Princess of Prussia".

"The Princess of Prussia" Renata Coleman – Hancock Family Photo

We danced for a bit and then she suggested that we go and sit down on a bench not far from the dance floor in a yard dimly lit by torches. We talked for a while, and the next thing I knew we were kissing. That's when I heard running footsteps and a weirdly anguished moaning coming toward us.

About the time I looked up, a guy slammed into us and knocked both of us and the bench over backward. To say the least, I was stunned and had no idea what was going on. She and I jumped up. He swung and hit her so hard he knocked her flat on her back.

I couldn't believe my eyes. The guy had the look of a madman. Normally, I would have attacked him, but I kept thinking about the promise I had made to my mother not to do anything to upset Vincent's daughter's wedding.

When the princess got up, he swung and knocked her flat again. I had never seen anything like it. I felt like I was in the twilight zone. But all of a sudden, I was myself again, thinking, *I'm sorry, Mother, I didn't start this, but I am damn sure going to finish it.*

Vincent and Jacqueline O'Brien in 1975 at the wedding of their daughter Susan to John Magnier. Their son David on the left – Magnier Family Photo

The princess got up again, screaming and cursing at him, "You goddamn sonofabitch, you dirty bastard," and a stream of words in German I couldn't understand.

I've never seen a woman so mad in my life. About that time, four Irishmen rushed over and grabbed the guy and asked him what the hell he thought he was doing. He was glaring at Renata and visibly shaking. He didn't say a word.

I wanted to go after him and told the Irish boys, "Turn this mother fucker loose." Thank God, they didn't. Vincent and some others showed up and told me to forget about it, that the guy was in love with the princess and had apparently been drinking heavily. That much I had come to understand by now. When mixed, love and whiskey can do strange things.

TRAVELIN'

♪

Through the fields I wandered, past the rocky creek
To the backstretch of my fathers farm
Then when I grew older I headed out to seek
The mystery of the lands far from my home

I crossed the blue Atlantic to visit London town
Went through the misty mountains of Switzerland
Sailed the sea to Norway to find what could be found
And many a thing I came to understand

Travelin', ain't nothing like being free
Roamin' with the wind through field and woods
Travelin' that's the life for me
I'd spend my days a ramblin' and travelin' if I could

I met a lot of people saw a lot of sights
Did a lot of things I'd never done
Roamed the wide world over from the valleys to the heights
In cold moonlight and in hot summer sun

My ramblin' days are over, and the work is hard and dull
I'm tied up and I cannot get away
By nature, I'm a rover and now I'm in a lull
But I hope to hit the road again someday

Travelin', ain't nothing like being free
Roamin' with the wind through field and woods
Travelin', that's the life for me
I'd spend my days a ramblin and travelin' if I could

In 1972, I met a girl from Germany named Maria who was visiting a family in Lexington. I thought I was in love again. When she went back to Germany, we wrote letters and I believed we might possibly get married. I went over for a visit and met her family in December. Then she and I went skiing in Bavaria at Garmisch-Partenkirchen.

Maria had been engaged to a German named Sepal before she came to the states, and the following August, nearly a year later, she sent me a letter saying she was going to get married in September. From the tone of the letter, I didn't think she really wanted to marry the guy and I decided that I just better make sure.

I talked this over with Adger who encouraged me to go to Germany. He said, "Arthur, if you don't go, you might regret it for the rest of your life."

I got to Frankfurt, Germany the night before the wedding and drove to Kassel, arriving after midnight and staying in a local hotel. At first light, I arrived in Maria's hometown of Dahlhausen and passed a church with a sign out front draped with flowers. It read, *Ave Maria.* It was where she was to be married later that afternoon.

I had seen the movie *The Graduate* and I guess I thought I could show up on the wedding day and get the same result as Dustin Hoffman, who ran away with the bride-to-be before her wedding.

Early that morning, I was outside her house throwing gravel and change from my pocket up at the window of the room I remembered as hers from my earlier visit. It was like Romeo and Juliet, but she didn't appear on the balcony.

A man opened the window and said, "Ja." At first, I thought it might be her fiancé, but it was her brother. I asked if Maria was there, and he said, "Ein moment." Her mother came to the door and invited me in for some brown bread and coffee. When her father saw me, he said, "Oh, mien Gott, Artua."

With Canadian rock and roll musician Ronnie Hawkins of The Band, Nashville music icon Fred Foster and
Maria Boker of Dahlhausen, Germany in 1972 – Lexington Herald Leader

Before Maria came downstairs, I could hear her father lecturing her in a loud voice about this being the day of the wedding. She entered the room and seemed happy to see me and wasn't terribly upset by my showing up on the very day she was to be married. Her father was another story. Later, he brought her a huge pill that I suspected was a tranquilizer and told her in German to "take this."

She had to be at the salon by nine that morning, so I drove her over. It was raining and we sat in the car and talked for a while. I asked her to come back to Kentucky and live on the farm with me instead of marrying the German.

She said, "Arthur, I love you. You are a gentleman, but I love Sepal, too. I am a German, and my father wants me to stay in Germany and marry a German. I must say no, I am so sorry."

We got out of the car and shared a last kiss. She walked to the door of the salon with tears in her eyes and waving goodbye, went inside and closed the door. It was sprinkling rain. I said to myself, "Well, so be it." I drove back to Frankfurt and caught the next plane to London.

I knew it was finished, over and done.

FINISHED OVER AND DONE

Gone are the blue eyes that once shone so bright
That cherished every move that you made in their sight
Gone is the warm smile at all that you'd say
No trace of the fair face that vanished away

Past are the days when the world was like spring
And lost are the days when your heart could only sing
At hand are those times that are colder than stone
When loneliness chills you right through to the bone

When you're feeling the hurtin', the pain and the burden
And no longer caring if tomorrow will ever come
When she's no longer near you to hold you and cheer you
It's finished, it's over and done

Sometimes it's a good world when things go your way
But for the most part it's a rough life all the way
And just when you think you're beginning to win
You come to find out that you lose in the end

You overlooked treasure while searching for trash
Now all that is left of your love is the ash
And as you sit trembling and pondering fault
The answer lies silently locked in time's vault

When you're feeling the hurtin', the pain and the burden
And no longer caring if tomorrow will ever come
When she's no longer near you to hold you and cheer you
It's finished, it's over and done

CHAPTER 8

Gettin' Drunk

ALCOHOLISM HAS ALWAYS been a mystery to me. It was years before I ever really understood what I was doing and why. My parents used to have a couple of drinks every night. One time, when I was a little boy, I wanted to taste a drink. They gave me one and said to take a big sip. I did and almost choked to death. It was straight bourbon and it burned my mouth.

I grew up thinking that whiskey was a great friend, comforter, and helper. It took a long time for me to finally realize that alcohol was not my friend but my worst enemy.

The first time I discovered the power of alcohol was the summer when I was fourteen on my way back to Kentucky from Woodberry on the train, the old George Washington. The Woodberry boys boarded in Orange, Virginia. The train was going to stop for a while in Charlottesville, so we found a liquor store and got an older guy to get us a fifth of Jack Daniel's.

I wanted to see what it was like to really get drunk. I started drinking the Jack Daniel's out of little paper cups like the cowboys in the movies downed jiggers. It would burn my throat and then I'd chase it with a cup of water. Well, I got absolutely destroyed. I remember trying to walk down the hall in the Pullman car and everything was spinning round and round. I was falling up against the walls and I went into Royden Peabody's room.

I asked Royden, "What am I going to do?"

He said, "Oh, just take the antidote. I have some here. Drink this fast."

I thought it was something like an Alka-Seltzer and remember seeing the glass about half full of this clear liquid.

He said, "Now, drink it real fast for it to have a good effect."

I turned it up and took a big gulp, and I remember it burning all the way down. It was straight gin he had given me.

That's the last thing I remember until the next morning. There was a pounding on my door and a loud voice outside saying, "Winchester, Winchester." It was the porter trying to get me up. The train was about to leave the station.

I didn't know where in the hell I was when I woke up and when I realized what had happened, I said, "Oh, my God."

I'd had my suit on from the night before. The coat was all wrinkled and I had thrown up on it. I took a hairbrush, knocked off some of the dried puke, and discovered I had also peed in my pants.

The porter was frantically calling, "Winchester, let's go, let's go, everybody off the train, come on! You the last one to get off!"

He got my big bag, and I got my guitar. I remember looking out from the platform and seeing all the parents greeting their sons and daughters who had already detrained. Then I spotted Mama and Daddy, and my sister, Clay. They were all smiles until they saw me coming down the steps. I was totally disheveled. When I looked a second time, my father was looking at me like he knew something wasn't right.

Mama came to give me a hug. She said, "Ahggg, my God, you smell like you've been in a pigsty."

When I went up to Daddy to shake hands, he scowled at me and angrily said, "Go get in the back, you goddamn dog."

It was an Oldsmobile station wagon, and they rolled the back window down. I sat back there all the way home, and nobody said a thing. When I got home, I remember Mama saying, "Ahhthuh, you go and get yoself cleaned up."

I went to my room and took a shower and went to sleep. I didn't wake up that afternoon until about four o'clock. I had found out exactly what it was like to get drunk.

Maybe that's what it would take for most people to learn, but for me it was just an appetizer. Daddy taught me to take responsibility and again repeated his axiom, "Be a man, Bud, be a man."

A man I was not yet, but a young fool I certainly had been. Like Sam Ransom used to say, "When you drinkin', you ain't thinkin'. When police cars start lookin' like little toys, and policemen start lookin' like little boys, you drinkin'! ain't you drinkin'!"

FREEDOM

Freedom gained is freedom lost
When being free increases cost
When life is filled with fear and dread
And hate and spite is in our head
When we lose our smile and zest
And never seem to do our best
When we think that life's a joke
And the answers lie in rum and coke.
When we change into someone
Who's like a convict on the run
And do things that we'd never do
Because they're never really you.

When all is lost is freedom found,
When we have let our loved ones down?
When we hurt and fight and fuss
With those who so depend on us?
When we risk death and mutilation
For our idea of a night's vacation.
And wake up sick to the morning sun
Not knowing what we've said or done?

Seeking freedom from our cares
Can bring to life our worst nightmares
And freedom's not what it may seem
In the haze and smoke of a drunkard's dream.
For freedom is a state of mind
That we perhaps may gain in time,
And if we're wise we'll heed and scorn
The freedom of John Barleycorn.

That was the first of many chapters. These episodes continued. Once I was in Lexington, riding down the street, talking to this girl, and I was so drunk that I stupidly threw a glass out the window. There was a cop behind me. They put me in jail.

The next morning, the bail bondsman came down the jail hallway. I was waking up on the floor on newspapers and heard a *rat-a-tat-tat* noise. He was rapping the bars with his cane, and calling out, "Gentlemens, gentlemens . . . in jail, need bail? See me, R. Tee."

Alcoholism starts out slowly. At first, drink seems to be our friend, and we have a lot of fun with it socially. But then we cross a mysterious line, and it becomes our enemy. We have passed our tolerance point.

I read something one time where a normal drinker will have a couple of drinks and his mood swings in the direction of euphoria. But the guy with the problem swings totally to euphoria. To keep that euphoria, he keeps drinking. The next day, he doesn't come back to normal; his mood swings to depression and he will need an *"attitude adjuster"* in the form of another drink.

Whereas the normal drinker might go out and have too much, he will only have a hangover the next day. He will merely write it off as just a big night on the town. He doesn't feel that terrible depression or remorse, only a headache.

And he doesn't do crazy things like riding a motorcycle into a pool during a party, or hitting a mounted moose in the nose and knocking him off the wall simply because he doesn't like the way the moose looks at him.

The year after I graduated from Vanderbilt with a BA in history, Daddy said the first thing he wanted me to do was learn how to train the horses we raised at Claiborne. So, he got me a job in New York

As a groom in the winners circle at Aqueduct Race Track – Hancock Family Photo

Working as an assistant to trainer Eddie Neloy at Belmont Park – Hancock Family Photo

with Eddie Neloy, who trained horses for the Phipps family that had boarded horses at Claiborne for decades. My nickname around the barn was "Hitchcock".

Once, I stayed out until four in the morning and had to be at the barn by six o'clock. I was so hung over I had to stick my head down in champion Buckpasser's water bucket. But at least I was there. I only missed one day the whole year. That's when I stayed in Manhattan partying with a girl I had met and had to call Mr. Neloy to tell him I couldn't make it by six and I was going to be late. I told him I was sorry and I would be there shortly.

He said, "Good morning, Hitchcock. Have you got something there with you?"—meaning a female companion—and when I said, "Yes, sir." He said, "Hitchcock, if you come in today, you're fired."

There were only a few times in my life I missed work from being out drinking all night when I should have been tending to business. Even if I had been out until three or four o' clock, I was very dedicated to being at work on time.

And I was. I was just that way. Daddy instilled that work ethic in me. He believed in duty and devotion. So, as hung over as I might be it was very rare for me to oversleep—and when I did, I was genuinely full of remorse. Normal people will have a couple of drinks and forget about it. They might have two Pepsi-Colas, but they're not going to drink twelve. Once I had a hangover and realized I'd had two six packs of beer the night before. I knew something was wrong. I was learning that I would lose control of the amount I drank, when I drank, sometimes.

If people ask me now why I don't drink, I just say, "I'm allergic to alcohol; I break out in a drunk." It took me some time to figure out that I also sometimes was just breaking out in Bull Hancock; like when I was trying to learn everything I could about horses; or working my ass off following his work ethic; and sometimes explosively losing my temper.

After going back to work at Claiborne in the summer of 1967, one of my first jobs was to go to Chicago to pick up the great Argentine stallion Forli who was coming to stud at the farm. My reputation had preceded me.

When I got to the barn, a lean, stern-faced guy in short sleeves with a bald head and the eyes and look of an eagle came out and walked aggressively right up to me. He had a fleur-de-lis tattoo on his arm.

He said, "You're a big sonofabitch. What are you doing here? You probably think you can fight a little."

I sort of backed away, thinking to myself, who the hell is this? I thought he might be some kind of nut.

I said, "Well, I've been known to . . ."

He then stuck out his hand, broke into a big smile, and said, "I'm Charlie Whittingham."

This was my introduction to one of greatest horse trainers of all time, who would ultimately become one of the most important people in my life as a mentor and dear friend. As we were shaking hands, the legendary Kentucky veterinarian, Alex Harthill, stepped out of the shadows with a grin on his face. Doc knew about my past and had talked to Charlie about playing a trick on me.

I had been working for Mr. Neloy in New York for about five months when, on my day off, I drove from Queens into Manhattan to visit some friends from Nashville who were working in a brokerage firm on Wall Street.

It was August and about 100 degrees. I was sweating, tired, and hungry, and couldn't find a parking place for my car, a white Pontiac convertible with no air conditioning and Kentucky tags. So, I drove around and around a three or four block area for about thirty minutes until finally one opened up.

As I was attempting to back into the spot, a Volkswagen shot in right behind me and took my parking place. I was instantly in a rage. I got out and there was a heavyset man about ten years older locking his door. He looked up at me with a cunning smile. "You gotta move fast in New Yahk, Kentuckian," he said.

The Bull Hancock in me knocked him backward and down into the middle of the street where he began squealing, "Help! Officuh! Help! Assault! Assault! Officuh!"

I jumped in my car, drove down to Greenwich Village where I parked, and then rode the subway back to East 68th Street to visit my friends.

A few years later, a guy approached me in Nashville's Printer's Alley one night where I was in line to see a show at one of the clubs. He complimented the long, wool overcoat my uncle had given me and said he was going to buy it. I said, "It's not for sale." He got mad and threatened to take it off of me. I left him holding his jaw and lying in the alley for his trouble.

Some years later, I still had a short fuse. Sullivan and I were at Steak and Ale restaurant in Lexington. There were a lot of nice families having dinner, when a bunch of noisy out-of-towners fresh from the Keeneland races came in and settled at a corner table.

They must have been celebrating even before, because they were boisterous and disruptive. One loudmouth more obnoxious than the rest began spewing extremely foul language like you might hear in the worst kinds of places. Every now and then words laced with profanity would ring out in his up-east accent to be heard by the entire crowd.

I looked around and there were young children there whose parents were becoming noticeably uneasy. By this time, the loudmouth had fired up a big, long cigar and was laughing and blowing stinking smoke everywhere.

I just lost it. I couldn't help myself. I jumped up and stormed toward his table. The guy saw me coming.

"Shut up, shut your goddamn mouth," I told him. Then I grabbed the cigar out of his mouth and stuffed it in his drink. I have never seen a more shocked look on a face before or since.

I was just waiting for him to say something when Paul came up behind me, put his hands on my shoulders and said, "Come on, Arthur, let's go, let's get outta here."

I stood there for a bit and when nobody at the table did anything, I walked on out with Paul. He said he glanced at two or three tables as we left, and all the parents had smiles on their faces, which he took for their approval.

Those were three times when I couldn't blame my behavior on liquor. And luckily, I didn't get arrested. Unfortunately, there were several more instances to come when that was not the case, and I ended up in a jail cell four times.

Alcoholism is a progressive disease that is genetic. We drink excessively because we are alcoholics. I learned the hard way that I can do some things successfully, but that I cannot drink successfully. Dr. Jekyll was a successful and highly respected physician, but one drink of that potion, and he became the notorious Mr. Hyde.

I'M NOT AN ALCOHOLIC,
I JUST LIKE GETTIN' DRUNK

Once I had a darlin' wife, a little girl and boy
A pretty house on pleasant street, life was full of joy
Then a strange thing came over me, like my mind was blown
Now I've lost my family and everything I own

She would always chew me out for goin' to the bars
Gettin' charged with DUIs and wreckin' the family cars
I spent a little time in a hospital and did a few nights in jail
But every time I tried to change, I always seemed to fail

But I'm not an alcoholic, I just like gettin' drunk
You think I got problems, hell, that's what my wife thunk
You can rave on about Al-Anon and talk all about AA
But if you buy me one more round, buddy, you'll make my day

Once I quit for seven months and never touched a drop
That's when I became convinced that I could always stop
Then I went down to the Boom Boom Room to have a beer and dance
Two or three days later, I come to in Paris, France

But I'm not an alcoholic, I just like gettin' drunk
You think I got problems, that's what my ex-wife thunk
You can rave on about Al-Anon and talk all about AA
But if you buy me one more round, buddy you'll make my day
If you buy me one more round, buddy, I'll set you straight

CHAPTER 9

Me and Paul

"It's been rough and rocky travelin'
But I'm finally standin' upright on the ground
After takin' several readings
I'm surprised to find my mind's still fairly sound

I guess Nashville was the roughest
But I know I've said the same about them all
We received our education
In the cities of the nation, me and Paul"
—WILLIE NELSON

PAUL SULLIVAN AND I met in a fistfight when we were in grade school and have been the best of friends ever since. I was twelve and he was eleven. I was in the seventh grade, and he was a new boy in my school. For some reason I didn't like him. I don't know why. I just didn't like him.

We were at football practice and learning handoffs. When he'd come through the line, I'd slam the ball into his stomach. When we were done, he was mouthing off to somebody that he was going to whip my ass for slamming the ball into him. I said the same thing about him. After we took showers, I came out and there he was with a couple of his buddies.

One said, "Sullivan wants to see you."

I said, "What for?"

Paul said, "I heard you was gonna whip my ass."

I said, "I am. I will."

A friend of ours named Bud Wells held his hand out and said, "Best man hit." Paul hit Bud's hand, and then he said to Paul, "Now, you hit him twice as hard."

Paul hit me right in the side of my head. I turned around and the fight was on. My father had taught me how to box, so I hit him back two or three times. He didn't know how and just kept swinging wildly. He had a lot of courage and we fought long enough for me to get tired. He landed a few punches. I had hit him several really good licks, so I said, "Have you had enough?"

He said, "If you have?"

When I was 14 and Paul was 13, we went to see triple horror shows at the movie theater in Paris. *Wolfman, Dracula,* and *Frankenstein* were the tripleheaders. The shows weren't over until midnight so I had asked my father earlier if the night watchman could pick us up. The moon was full that night and Daddy said we should just walk the one mile home. The shows scared the holy hell out of both of us and I wasn't looking forward to it, especially after watching Wolfman tear people to shreds under the full moon.

We began to walk hurriedly out the Winchester Road toward Claiborne House, where Paul was spending the night with us.

Just as we were passing the stallion paddocks at Claiborne, one of the stallions closest to us on the other side of the hedge row suddenly snorted loudly. Paul and I must've jumped 10 feet forward, but by the time I hit the ground, I knew from experience what the noise was. Paul didn't.

Paul was ahead of me because he had taken off running full speed down the road. So, to scare Paul I screamed, "Ohhh no, ohhh please stop, no, help!" I let out one more anguished, groaning scream and then stood still. I could hear him running and about every tenth step I could hear him sobbing, "Ohhhhhh God, Ohhhhh God."

He was totally terrified. He thought that the monster had gotten me and was now coming for him. I watched him run in the moonlight all the way up the driveway to the house and then bound up the front steps in two leaps. I have never seen anyone cover ground so fast in my life.

I jogged on back to the house, and when I got to the stairs leading down to my room in the basement, I slowly stomped on each step while making a low, growling sound. When I got to the door of my room, Paul was trembling under the covers peering out from under the sheets. I couldn't stop laughing and he was still shaking. The story of the Wolfman has become a local legend.

About a year later, we decided we would go into Xalapa Farm, which had "Keep Out" and "Posted" signs all over the front. People around Paris had said whatever you do don't ever go into that place. The custodian up there was a mean, bad sonofabitch. They said he was not a man to mess with because he had already been in prison for killing two men.

The farm was surrounded by a large stone wall and the only way in was through large forbidding gates made out of heavy walnut timber. I had ridden my Vespa motor scooter, scouting around the outskirts of the farm several times and had noticed that one of the gates was sometimes left open.

In the middle of this farm, there was a huge stone tower resembling something out of the Middle Ages and rising up one hundred feet in the air. I became obsessed with going up into that tower and seeing the view. So, I looked up the caretaker's number in the phonebook and gave him a call to request permission to see it. Of course, I didn't tell him who I was. His answer was brief and hateful, "Don't nobody never come in hyar." Then he hung up on me. Right then, I made my mind up I was going to get into that tower, and I told my pal Paul about my plan. He was as adventurous as I was, so one hot summer day we rode the Vespa up to the farm to see if the gate was possibly open. Lo and behold it was, and I drove the motor scooter into the farm and pulled it up into the middle of a cornfield located near the tower.

The scooter was totally concealed by the corn. We had even gone to the trouble to fluff up the grass on the outside of the cornfield where we entered off the farm road. After we listened for a while and figured the coast was clear, we sneaked up to the tower. There was a stone house located about one hundred yards from it but there were no cars around and we didn't think anyone was there.

I tried in vain to open the door, but it had a lock on it. I was nervous as hell that we had gotten this close and couldn't get in, so I picked up a large rock nearby and hit the lock hard three times until it finally came off the hinge. The banging made a loud noise, so Paul and I went back and hid in the cornfield for five minutes or so to make sure nobody came around.

Then we went into the tower and slowly climbed the spiraling iron staircase. About halfway to the top, a bevy of bats flew out and scared the hell out of us. It was eerie and spooky in there but, undaunted, we continued to climb. When we reached the top, there was one of the most gorgeous views I'd ever seen. From our vantage point one hundred feet high, we could see the entire countryside for miles around, which encompassed most of bucolic Bourbon County. It was breathtaking.

We spent a few minutes up in the tower checking things out and then nervously headed back down to get the hell out of there. We reached the bottom and listened quietly to make sure the coast was clear and then started out the door. All of a sudden from behind a large tree, there stepped the caretaker with a giant .45-caliber pistol in his hand, pointed and waving right at us.

He said, "God damn you, what the hell you doin' hyar?"

I said, "Sir, Billy and Bobby Mclhenny from Winchester told us to come on over and it would be fine to go up in the tower with them. They told me they had permission from you, and it would be just fine."

He said, "Whur they at?"

I said, "Sir, they're right up there in the tower." That was some of the fastest thinking I had ever done.

He said, "Y'all wait rat hyar!"

Then he ran into the tower holding his gun. As soon as he disappeared, I took off running with Paul right beside me. We hurdled a barbwire fence and tore down through the corn as fast as we could go with the shucks cutting our face and skin as we went until we reached the scooter. I cranked it but it wouldn't start, and I thought we were dead. My heart was about to jump out of my chest. On about the fifth crank the motor purred away and I gunned it. We went flying through the rows of corn toward the gate.

Thank God we got out of there. With Paul looking behind us all the way, I went full speed back down to Claiborne House and drove the scooter up to the swimming pool. Safe and realizing what we had done, we started laughing and celebrating the success of one hell of an adventure.

But when we jumped into the pool, we got the punishment we had earned. We were both covered with sweat and had cuts all over us from running and riding through the corn—so the chlorine in the water stung like fire on every cut we had sustained.

PART FOUR

IN THE BACKYARD

One of the happiest times that I've had,
Was in the backyard cooking steaks with Dad.
The dogs lying near and the sun going down,
Fresh fallen leaves were all on the ground.

Just us together, a boy and a man,
Alone by the fire, a drink in our hand.
He gazed out over the fields and said,
This will be yours, Bud, after I'm dead.

I've worked very hard, most all of my days,
For you children and Mother, and, old bud, it pays.
So you do your best, Son, when you are the boss,
Or all that I've worked for will surely be lost.

I may not succeed, Dad, but if ever you die
I'll promise you one thing, I'm going to try.

CHAPTER 10

Dynasty Detour

SOME OF THE MOST important things in my life happened in the backyard at Claiborne House when Daddy was grilling steaks for the family, which he loved to do. There was the time when he knocked me down for arguing over the speed of Sputnik. Then there was the night he told me about some of his Princeton classmates who, though much smarter than he was, had ended up as failures through lack of ambition or discipline. Most important of all, however, was the night when he told me outright that Claiborne was my destiny.

"You know, Bud, I could retire right now," he said. "The only reason I'm still working is for you children. One day, you and Seth will be running this place but now you need to be out there with the men, just like a good officer in the battle."

Then he repeated his old axiom, "The only real happiness in life is a job well done."

So that's what I always did—the best job I could. I would get up and foal mares in the middle of freezing winter nights. I'd muck out stalls, cut weeds, mow, and put up hay. I was out there on the farm, boots on the ground, working my tail off with the other guys.

Even though I had my mind on other things, like girls and guitars, I knew early on what I was expected to do. That's why Daddy kept trying to teach me what I would need to know.

With Seth and Daddy in the Saratoga paddock, August of 1969 – Keeneland Library Collection

When I was just a little boy, Daddy would have me hold the tools for the blacksmith and then later teach me how to trim if a horse is toeing out or in, or if he was offset at the knees. You need to know what to do, from the bottom to the top. He taught me good conformation from bad and how to look for the little things.

He always used a quote from *Poor Richard's Almanac* by Benjamin Franklin. "For the want of a nail, the shoe was lost; for the want of a shoe the horse was lost; and for the want of a horse the rider was lost, being overtaken and slain by the enemy, all for the want of care about a horseshoe nail."

He'd have me study bloodlines from which the great stallions had descended and tell me how my grandfather bought only broodmares from families with an established record of producing winners. He also said, "for a deal to be a good deal, it has to be good for both parties." Most of all, he taught me the importance of a great work ethic.

One time when I was still at Vanderbilt and supposed to work the summer at Claiborne, I went to Michigan with some guys and fell in love. I was supposed to be at work on June twenty-first, but I called on the twentieth and asked Daddy if I could put off my starting date a few days.

He said, "You're supposed to be at work on the twenty-first. That's the deal, the verbal contract you made, and when you report to a man for work, you come when you're supposed to be there. You get back down here and come to work."

By the time I went to work for Mr. Neloy years later, that Bull Hancock work ethic was deeply embedded. I started out walking hots and riding the vans with horses between Belmont and Aqueduct. We started at 6:00 sharp in the morning and sometimes worked till late at night.

I was still in shape from swimming and working on the farm, so I could handle Buckpasser, who was one of the best horses ever raised at Claiborne. He was a sonofabitch to handle. After he worked or galloped, especially when he came back from a race, he'd jump four feet off the ground, kick, and carry on. So, that's why they'd pick me to walk him—because they knew I could handle him. He tried to get away from me two or three times. It scared me because the last thing I wanted to do was be the man who let Buckpasser loose to get hurt. He never did.

Half the battle of leading a horse is to keep him calm. Don't look him in the eye. That's threatening to him. He is a flight animal.

You have a hunter's eye. So, look straight ahead and try to calm him down, like you would a dog that's growling at you.

Just talk and say something like, "Come on, son. Whoa now! What's the matter with you today? Come on." And you can jerk the shank a little and get into him just like you would a kid that's getting out of line, then give him a little relief.

That year with Neloy was a good one. We won a lot of big races. I worked hard. It was seven days a week. It was a great experience where I learned even more about horses.

I remember when Bold Lad was there. I had to tub him every day, which entailed having him stand still in a tub of ice water. I would give him carrots and eventually get him to where he would nicker for them. I did this day after day for a couple of months. I would say "Carrot?" and wait for him to respond. Finally, he learned to nicker at the word, and I'd give him his carrot.

They always told me horses have a memory like an elephant. Bold Lad left the track in March and went to stud at Claiborne. I didn't get back to the farm until later that August. When I got there, I went to see him, and I took a carrot with me and stayed downwind so he wouldn't smell it. I could tell he recognized me and when he looked at me, I said, "Carrot?" And he nickered.

Horses are smart. A horse is a lot more complicated creature than most people imagine. I think that a lot of horses could run as fast as Sunday Silence and other champions, but some just have that will to assert themselves and others don't, just like with people. Some are leaders and some are followers.

I once mentioned to Daddy an article I read by Leon Rasmussen, who was an advocate of inbreeding as a method of raising winning horses. Daddy thought I was in agreement with his theory.

"Well, you and Mr. Rasmussen are both brilliant men," he said. "Neither one of you ever bred a good horse."

He believed outcrossing was the way to get the best horses. He told me about breeding fruit flies in his genetics class at Princeton, and how those that were inbred had no vitality or hybrid vigor. That's why he brought those stallions in from Europe. There was no Nearco blood in American breeding when he imported Nasrullah, and now it stands as the cross that produced dozens of great horses, including Secretariat.

My father taught me so much, but it always had to be his idea. The first instance I remember had to do with "creep" feeding. There were little pens in the pastures with the top board too low for the mares to get under, but just high enough off the ground for the foals to get in and eat their grain out of the trough.

One year, we had two foals cut their heads trying to get into the creeps at night. I suggested to Daddy maybe we should feed them the first time on a moonlit night when they could see better.

With Daddy inspecting a new stallion at Claiborne – Keeneland Library Collection

"Well, you're a brilliant man, Arthur," he said. "You thought of it, but I never thought of it and your grandfather never thought of it and your great-grandfather never thought of it, but you did. You're a brilliant man."

About two or three months later when the *BloodHorse Magazine* was interviewing him about the practice of creep feeding, he told them, "We always creep feed the foals the first time around a full moon, which minimizes the risk of injury."

Obviously, he had appreciated my contribution—but he never wanted to give me any credit, which is the same way my mother said he had been treated by my grandfather.

When my year with Eddie Neloy in New York was up, I returned to Claiborne to help manage and break the yearlings and later became the assistant broodmare manager. I did that for three years, but then Daddy put me through the same test my grandfather had given him.

When he was about the same age, his own father had sent him to manage Ellerslie Farm in Charlottesville, Virginia. He told him to make a profit or go do something else. It was the same thing Daddy told me when he sent me to manage a small farm up the road from Claiborne. He advised me about buying a couple of broodmares and said if I made a profit, he would hire me back, and if I couldn't, well, "Good luck."

I went up and lived in a little house on a hundred acres I leased from Claiborne. I did all the mowing and horse work myself. Things were going pretty good, and I started getting a few clients, like my friend Bobby Russell, who wrote the songs *Honey, Little Green Apples,* and *The Night the Lights Went Out in Georgia.* John sent me a mare. Over the next couple of years, Daddy took me with him to Saratoga. We'd go out to dinner with people, and I thought he was just beginning to feel and act differently toward me.

Back in 1969, before I had my wreck, he and I were at the Saratoga Sale, staying together in a private club called The Reading Room. There was a television in our room and Walter Cronkite came on the nightly news and began showing different pictures of everything going on at Woodstock, the rock and roll festival, which was in full swing that August.

CBS showed scenes of every kind of hippie and beatnik imaginable. They were smoking dope, hallucinating, and dancing around or rolling in the mud to the sound of Jimi Hendrix. There were lots of scantily clad wild-looking girls, who were also either dancing half naked or making out with the bearded, unkempt hippies.

All the people were about my age. Woodstock was only about a hundred miles away, and I was a big fan of Jimi Hendrix so I made the comment that I might drive over there and check it out. I also wanted to hear Joe Cocker and Crosby, Stills & Nash. Daddy gave me a look as if to say you must have lost your mind and then said, "Goddamned dirty, filthy sons of bitches! One small, well-placed atom bomb would solve half the problems we've got in this country!"

I believe Daddy's view of me and my music began to change a few years before he died, when he met Fred Foster at a Kentucky Derby party at Claiborne House where I had taken him as my guest.

Fred loved the horses and was anxious to go and meet my parents. But I warned him in advance that Daddy wouldn't like him because he didn't like music people and because Fred wore a toupee. Daddy didn't think much of bald men who wore toupees.

My grandmother had passed down to all of us a story that might have had something to do with Daddy's sensitivity about baldness.

One time the Lion of Hollywood, Louis B. Mayer, came to Claiborne to buy some horses. The first thing he noticed displayed in the living room was a photograph of a handsome young man.

He asked my grandmother who it was. She told him that was her son, who would be arriving any minute to take him out on the farm and show him the horses for sale.

Mr. Mayer said he was looking forward to meeting him because "a man who looks like that could be just the one I'm looking for to cast in my new movie." But that was an old picture and my father had since lost all his hair. When Daddy walked in to meet him, Mr. Mayer didn't even mention the man in the photo or ever again entertain the idea of inviting bald Bull Hancock to Hollywood.

I don't know if the famous movie mogul bought any horses from Claiborne that day, but several decades later his continuing interest in the Kentucky breeding industry would significantly impact the life and business of another balding Arthur B. Hancock—me.

But my father's previous disdain for his own hair loss and for anyone who wore a toupee had obviously diminished. I was stunned when the week after the Derby my father told me how much he liked Fred.

"He's got a good eye," Daddy said, using a phrase we all use in judging horseflesh. "The eye is the window to the soul. And the Lord writes with a legible hand. Fred is a good man."

For five days in August 1972, I was again with my father at Saratoga. We went to the races together every day, and each night attended the Fasig-Tipton Yearling Sales at seven. Afterward, we would have dinner with friends or clients. It felt like the first time in many years that there was no friction between us. I had been making some progress in trying to quit drinking until I paid off my note at the bank.

Daddy said he admired that, and for the very first time he seemed to be proud of my accomplishments in music.

One night when we went to dinner, he told the CEO of Johnson & Johnson, the president of the L&N Railroad, and the head of a large New York bank that he was proud of me because the great Ray Price had recorded a couple of songs I had written, and Grandpa Jones who was a big star at the time, had recorded one I wrote called *Nashville On My Mind*. Daddy had seen him singing it on *Hee Haw* and said, "Damn, that show goes all over the world." He was right, and I got some good royalties from those cuts.

Among our dinner companions one of those nights was Sam Fleming, a rags-to-riches success who went from a three-dollar-a-night runner to become the legendary president of Third National Bank in Nashville, president of the American Bankers Association, and thirty-year trustee of Vanderbilt University. My father always respected accomplishment and had deliberately put me in the presence of other men who had succeeded as he had. I was rather startled when he told them that the music business was apparently as tough as the horse business and that I had had some success in what I had always loved to do.

He often told me, "You can't do two things and do either one well. You've got to make your mind up which one you want to do." And I had finally made my mind up for the horse business. I now played music as a hobby.

Daddy left Saratoga and went to visit Vincent O'Brien in Ireland to see some Claiborne partnership horses and go pheasant hunting. After he'd been there a couple of days, he woke up one morning with a 102-degree fever. Still feeling poorly two days later, he was told by a doctor that he was uncertain about what was bothering him. Jack Mulcahy, who was president of Pfizer Pharmaceutical at the time, flew Daddy to Vanderbilt Hospital in Nashville on his private plane.

I felt that Daddy and I were never closer than during those last three weeks. One day, I was alone with him in his hospital room when he had to get out of bed and rush to the bathroom. He didn't make it. So, I got a towel and was on my knees cleaning up. He said, "Bud, you don't need to do that. The nurse will come in here . . ."

He was watching me and tears welled up in his eyes. I knew by the look he gave me how he felt toward me. It was different than ever before. Over the last couple of weeks, we had spent together, our relationship was changing. I was earning his respect. Even through all of our past conflicts, I had known he loved me as his son, but in this moment, I could feel it man to man.

My father did not improve. In fact, his symptoms got worse. Dr. Josh Billings, one of my father's best friends with whom he had gone to Princeton, recommended exploratory surgery.

The day before the operation, my mother and my brother and sisters and I went down to Nashville to visit him. It was a sad and depressing day, and as soon as we arrived at his hospital room, we gathered around, and we all gave him a hug. We were very worried. He was lying on his back, propped up by some pillows, and was very pale and sallow. I thought his condition had deteriorated since I had seen him the week before.

There was a sense of urgency in his tone as he called us closer to his bedside. We all knew that he was going to bring up some very serious matters about the future.

There was a friendly nurse in the room, and no sooner had we all said hello than Daddy asked her to please leave the room because he had some business matters that he wanted to discuss with his family. Probably from a sense of denial or from trying to remain hopeful, my mother said, "Oh no, Bull, please not now. This can all wait until you are better."

I instinctively wanted to contradict my mother and say that we all needed to speak together right then, but probably for the same reasons I didn't say a word. The nurse stayed and the family talked about different things and tried to be positive. After about an hour, we left and went to spend the night with my mother's sister, Aunt Katie, and her husband, David Keeble.

When they opened up my father's abdomen, they found that he was eaten up with pancreatic cancer and closed him up. When he regained consciousness, Dr. Billings was by his side and told him the terrible news.

Daddy said, "Josh, how long do I have?"

Dr. Billings said, "Bull, it's bad. You've got maybe two weeks; maybe two months, at the most."

Daddy said, "Well, Josh, we'll try to make it two years."

He died two weeks later.

Over the years since, I have wondered a thousand times what my father was going to say that fateful day. I believed then and now that he was going to bring up changing his will to be more specific about how he wanted Claiborne to be run in the future. His will had been written back in 1967 when he still considered us boys. Seth was only seventeen, and I was just twenty-four.

He had even started talking about amending his will one night at dinner a week before we went to Saratoga. He said that when he got back from his trip, he planned to make changes and would already have done it had he known that Uncle Sam Clay, one of the trustees, intended to support "that damn liberal George McGovern in the presidential race."

If on that day in the hospital, he had asked Seth and me to carry on and run Claiborne together, I am certain that I would have stayed until hell froze over, no matter what.

Daddy died on September 14, 1972.

Adger happened to be in town that night and we went down to Claiborne House to cook steaks with my sister, Dell. Seth was married then to his first wife, Ellen. We all got along well but we didn't see much of each other. Seth was working at Claiborne while I was still up the road on my hundred leased acres I'd been managing the last couple of years.

Knowing Daddy was gravely ill and getting worse, I was walking out in the yard in front of Claiborne House. All the dogs were out there and running around. Dell came out and she was in tears.

"Arthur, Daddy died," she said, and just broke down.

I gave her a hug and with tears in my eyes went to the kitchen and got some steaks. I took them out to the grill where my dad and I had spent so many wonderful times together. I felt like my world had ended. I was looking out over the fields when, suddenly, out of nowhere, I felt this presence coming in toward me—coming in from the south. I didn't hear anything, didn't see anything, but I could just feel this weird onrushing energy hovering around me. I couldn't describe it, and still can't. It was otherworldly.

I'll never forget standing there and saying out loud, "My God, he's here. Daddy's here."

I thought I must be in shock because, while I heard no sound, in my mind I heard him plainly say these exact words: "Bud, I'm all right. You go on and do your best and I'll see you later."

Then I noticed the dogs. Two of them were lying flat—cowering, wild-eyed, shaking. The other was slinking slowly and silently back toward the house with his tail between his legs and his head low to the ground.

My father shortly before his death at age 62 – Hancock Family Photo

The service was at Claiborne House. Sullivan and Adger were there. Chris Williams and Bill Shwab came. We were all together then, four of my very best and closest friends. This meant the world to me.

Some said that it was like a state funeral. US senators, congressmen and the governor were there, the chairman of Superior Oil, the CEO of Pfizer, Bunker Hunt, Mr. Phipps, and Mr. Perry.

People came in from France, England, and Ireland to pay their respects. The pallbearers took the casket, and the large procession wended its way into town, through the streets of Paris and out to the cemetery. The streets were lined with people as we were driving toward the cemetery. I was sitting beside Mama and tightly squeezed her hand as we came to the gravesite.

They buried Daddy right beside Granddaddy and Grandmother.

Later, we went back up to the little house on the farm that I was leasing, just me and my close friends. That's one of the few times I ever saw Paul get out of hand. He got destroyed that night. I have often wondered about the emotional intensity that makes someone get dead drunk. I've only seen him do that two or three times over the years. It got to Paul. It got to all of us. It had been a rough day.

My reaction came a few days later. I remember stopping in a secluded place on the farm and sitting there shaking and crying like a baby for a long time. I kept saying over and over to myself, "He's gone, Daddy's gone." I couldn't believe it, and it all happened just as we were beginning to get along well. Years later, my feelings were perfectly summed up by a line in the song *The Leader of the Band*:

> *"I thank you for the kindness*
> *And the times when you got tough*
> *And, Papa, I don't think I said*
> *'I love you' near enough . . ."*
> —DAN FOGELBERG

The only time I ever saw my own father cry was the night after his dad had passed away. Daddy said a blessing before dinner and closed it by saying, "Lord, may Dad rest in peace. He was the finest man I ever knew." Then he broke down, and with his chest heaving, silently sobbed for several minutes as we all bowed our heads.

Daddy's will appointed three trustees and decreed that they follow the advice of three advisors he believed to be expert in the horse business. Two of these advisors, Bill Perry and Ogden Phipps, were important clients and his partners in many of the horses boarded on the farm. The third was his friend, Charlie Kenney, who was manager of another farm in Bourbon County.

After Daddy died, I went back to work at Claiborne. The advisors dictated that Seth and I divide our responsibilities with me in charge of the sales, the yearlings, and farm maintenance. Seth was designated to oversee the stallions and the broodmares.

The advisors also ordered that we should have a dispersal of the racing stock and the yearlings.

Mr. Perry owned half interest in many of the latter. In October, when I was already getting the horses ready to sell, we were having lunch with Mr. Phipps at Claiborne. In the middle of it, Bunker Hunt, who was a client, big-time owner, and oilman at the time, called me and offered us an opportunity to syndicate Bold Reasoning.

He wanted to do it in thirty-three shares and keep a third, or eleven shares, for himself. Seth and I liked the horse and thought this was a good deal for Claiborne, but Mr. Phipps threw a fit, raised his voice, and said, "All stallions at Claiborne will be syndicated in thirty-two shares!"

ARE YOU SLEEPING DADDY DARLING

Are you sleeping Daddy Darling
Is your kind old soul at rest
Are you alright in your new world
Daddy, you deserve the best

All our lives you made us happy
Gave us everything you could
And when the whole world seemed against us
You were always there and understood

Are you sleeping Daddy Darling
In your new home way up on high
Don't be lonesome for us Daddy
Some old day we'll see you by and by

I can still remember in the old days
How the work was hard and times were lean
When Mama did her best with all us children
And you went off to war for our country

Are you sleeping Daddy Darling
You know we think about you by the hour
And every time our thoughts are with you Daddy
We feel so very proud that you were ours
Oh Daddy we feel so very proud that you were ours

Reluctantly, I had to call Mr. Hunt back and tell him. After a long pause, he said that it would be okay. Mr. Hunt had only recently been on the cover of *Time Magazine* as the world's richest man. Bold Reasoning went on to sire the great Seattle Slew, a Triple Crown winner and superb stallion.

I felt humiliated to have to ask him. Why would one share be so important to make us almost lose the deal? Maybe it was just two silverbacks competing, one trying to get the better of the other. Or maybe it was because Mr. Hunt was my friend.

Whatever the reason, I knew I could not live my life under this sort of supervision and domination. Mr. Hunt had as many mares at Claiborne as Mr. Phipps at the time and I was embarrassed.

But the Phipps family name was nearly as deeply embedded in the history of Claiborne as our own. One member or another had been associated with most of the farm's famous horses since the 1920s when Mr. Phipps's mother and uncle formed Wheatley Stables. They bred and sold Seabiscuit, who was born and raised on the farm, as well as Bold Ruler, the sire of Secretariat and the grandsire of Seattle Slew.

This long association had given the Phipps family an unusually powerful, and not always welcome, influence on life at Claiborne. Mr. Phipps, for example, developed a habit of calling in the middle of dinner. He had to know when we would be sitting down for dinner each night, and Nathan regularly had to come and call my father away from the table to answer the phone. The conversations were often so lengthy, twenty minutes or more, that Daddy's dinner would have to be stashed in the oven. It made Mama furious, and she would often complain about it.

But Daddy always took the call and said nothing about it. It happened so often that both Seth and I vowed we would never have our dinner interrupted to talk about horses. In my opinion, Mr. Phipps knew he had his thumb on Claiborne and knew exactly what he was doing. I felt sorry for my father. I remember having dinner at the Phipps estate on Long Island once and seeing the white-coated servants with napkins folded over their arms and nobody calling Mr. Phipps away to talk on the phone.

Mr. Phipps had bought a number of horses from Colonel E.R. Bradley and formed his own stable in 1932. He was among the elite group of breeders that helped my father acquire and import Nasrullah from Ireland in 1950, a year before he was named champion sire of Europe. Nasrullah carried the first blood of the great Nearco available to breeders in North America and was five-time leading sire while standing at Claiborne.

But like Daddy, Mr. Phipps had never won the Kentucky Derby, and his best racehorse up to that point had been Buckpasser, the tough-to-handle champion I used to help take care of when I worked for Mr. Neloy.

The Phipps fortune came from the Carnegie steel empire and most of the family members were connected one way or another to the Bessemer Trust, which Mr. Phipps was managing when Daddy died. He was a powerhouse—and he knew it.

Mr. Perry belonged in the same category. Son of a Wall Street broker, he had married into the family of James Ben Ali Haggin, who had gone from Harrodsburg, Kentucky to strike it rich in the California gold rush. He had become a prominent Thoroughbred owner whose descendants helped found Keeneland.

When it came to selling all of the horses, Mr. Perry seemed obsessed with getting the fillies checked for breeding soundness before they left the racetracks.

"That's fine," I said. "We'll just need to announce at the sale that they're all sound for breeding. There's no rush."

That was how our veterinarian saw it, too.

But Mr. Perry kept hounding me, calling every couple of days.

Mr. Perry was the one advisor who insisted that all the yearlings be sent up to Fasig-Tipton Sales Company in New York to be sold. I strongly felt that they should stay in Kentucky. My father would have rolled over in his grave had he known that those yearlings weren't going to be sold at Keeneland, which his father helped found and where Daddy had been one of the three trustees.

So, at a big meeting of the family, the advisors, and the executors, I got up and left the room to call George Swinebroad at Keeneland. He agreed to put them in a special catalogue at their November Sale, which my father would have absolutely wanted.

When I came back in to the meeting and reported Keeneland's offer, Mr. Perry snapped at me, "Arthur, you're a hothead. These yearlings are going to be sold in New York!"

I looked at him and he was wearing an infuriating smirk. Right then and there, I decided I could not work under these circumstances. To me, Mr. Perry was an old blowhard. He was conceited and pompous. It was easy to understand why with all his inherited money he had accumulated five wives. The way he sat around stroking his corgi smoking from a silver cigarette holder made my flesh crawl. I ended up nicknaming him "the cat stroker". One thing was for sure—I did not want to work for him.

He obviously didn't like me either, so when I went down to Nashville to visit Fred at his recording studio in November, just for a day off after working two months without one, Mr. Perry complained about it. "There goes Arthur running off to Nashville again," he grumbled. "Those music people!" He brought that up with several others. I knew that, because Seth told me. My sister, Clay, had also heard Mr. Perry trashing my performance. I felt like I was in a straitjacket.

The disagreement with Mr. Phipps over the number of shares in Bold Reasoning, as well as Mr. Perry's complaint about my going to Nashville and demanding that we sell the horses in New York kept me unsettled and angry. They both wanted to be my master and ruler, and that wasn't going to happen.

Insisting that we sell those yearlings in New York was the straw that broke the camel's back, so I confided to Mama that I planned to leave Claiborne and go out on my own. I should have left right then and there, but she talked me out of it and begged me to wait until after the sale in New York. We needed to go there as a family, she insisted, to present a unified front until the horses were all sold.

Staying was a big mistake on my part because the night before the horses were sold, I went into New York City, got drunk, met a gorgeous girl, and didn't make it back to the sale barn at Belmont Park until 7:30 the next morning—when I should have been there at six. I am sure this didn't sit well with Mr. Phipps and Mr. Perry at all. But I already knew I'd be leaving Claiborne anyway. In hindsight, and with all due respect to those gentlemen, I gave them the ammunition they needed for what was about to occur and for what I had had in mind anyway.

The big meeting with the trustees and the advisors was held at the office at Claiborne a few weeks later. It was Mama, Seth, Clay, me—and them.

Before the meeting, Mr. Phipps remarked in an off-hand manner that every ship needs a captain, and Seth had actually told me a couple of days before what was going to happen. He and I were coming back from lunch when he blurted out, "Well, they're going to make me president."

I said, "What do you mean, Seth?"

He said, "That's what Mr. Phipps and Mr. Perry want to do."

"They told you that?"

He said, "Yeah." Just like that.

I had been trained by the best. I was older and much more experienced than Seth and had run my own farm. Now, they had hatched a plan to get me out. I didn't want to be a part of working for them anyway.

When, during the meeting, Mr. Phipps brought up again about a ship needing a captain, we got into a big discussion. I told them Daddy's will was there in the desk drawer and offered to get it out and read it to them. "In Daddy's will, it says that the executors are to follow the advice of the advisors," I said. "Is this what the advisors want?"

Only Phipps and Perry wanted it. Mr. Kenney had known me all my life. He was a good horseman and knew I was one, too. But in the presence of these two giants of the Turf, at first he raised no objection. And, so, the majority ruled.

Again, I told them all what my father's will said and that was the way it was going to be.

I said, "We know what the advisors think and I'm resigning my position with Claiborne Farm."

Then Mama broke in and said, "No, no, no. I don't want it to be that way. Just make me the captain, make me the president, and Arthur and Seth will be the vice presidents."

Homer Drew, the executor for First Security Bank, said, "Oh yes, Arthur, we can work this out."

Then executor Doug Parrish said, "Aw— Oh no, Bud, we want you all to work together. That's what your daddy wanted."

My uncle, Sam Clay, the third executor and a kind man, said, "Oh no, Arthur. That will destroy the family."

And finally, Charlie Kenney spoke up and said he thought Seth and I should run it together.

I heard an anguished kind of gasping from Mama, a very uncomfortable and emotional sound.

But Phipps and Perry paid them no attention. Through it all, Seth sat silently. But that is his nature. He was only twenty-three years old, my baby brother. He knew these men were the two biggest pillars of Claiborne.

To me, Mr. Phipps and Mr. Perry had acted secretly and slyly. They told Seth in advance what they were planning but kept it all from me. Mr. Phipps knew that making Seth president and demoting me would force me out. And with me out of the way, the advisors would naturally have more influence.

I thought, if that's how they feel, fine. I'm not going to hang around if I'm not wanted. Paul always said that while technically I wasn't fired, in essence I really was. He said they call it constructive discharge—demote someone and they'll leave.

It was all over. This was my exit from Claiborne, right then, right there. I said, "Y'all run it like you want to. You don't need me anymore. I'm out. Good luck to you; there's no need for me to hang around here." And I left before the meeting was over.

I had once thought I might want to be an explorer. Now I was going to explore life.

I remember striding down the hall through that office and out that door. I got in my Claiborne Farm station wagon to leave for the last time. I was shattered. But I knew I had done the right thing, even though it was the hardest thing I had ever done. I was giving up my heritage and my birthright. I thought, *now you'll at least find out what you're going to do in this life and whatever it is, you'll do it on your own.*

Ricky Nelson said it best in his song, *The Garden Party*: "It's alright now. I've learned my lesson well. You see, you can't please everyone, so you got to please yourself."

Ogden Phipps - Keeneland Library Collection

William Haggin Perry — Keeneland Library Raftery Turfotos Collection

CHAPTER 11

Leaving Claiborne

IT WAS ONLY NATURAL that the minute I resigned from Claiborne, Sullivan was the first person I wanted to talk to after doing what he had warned me would be crazy.

I drove into Paris with tears streaming down my cheeks and stopped at a phone booth to call him. "Do you want to meet me down at Hall's on the River? I just resigned."

Paul was shocked and said "Oh my God. You must be joking. You did what? Surely to God, you didn't."

At Hall's that night, I got drunk. We were sitting there, and I was really into the beer. Paul said, "What in the hell are you going to do now? I guess you're just going to be a bum."

I said, "No, I'm not gonna be a bum, Sullivan."

He said, "Yeah, you are. All you want to do is chase women, drink, and play that guitar!"

I looked at him with tears in my eyes. I said, "Paul, one day, I'm gonna win the Kentucky Derby and be bigger than Claiborne."

He gave me a sad glance and as she was passing by said, "Waitress, bring this fool another Budweiser."

It happened just like that.

I knew that's what I wanted to do. It was to be my life's dream. The Derby had eluded my father and I wanted to do it for him as well as for myself. But I thought winning it might take me until I was an old man—if I would ever be lucky enough to do it at all.

Deep down, I knew I could never rival Claiborne as far as the top stallions or the world-famous reputation.

Half the time, I had my doubts. I thought I might be going crazy. I would sit in the swing on the porch of that little house on my hundred leased acres, picking around on the guitar and thinking, maybe you are just a damn fool.

IF IT'S ALL THE SAME TO YOU

If it's all the same to you
I'll be leavin' in the mornin'
I'll be going to some different place
It's all I know to do.
I have thought the whole thing through
And I can feel the doubt abornin'
And I'll be leavin' in the mornin'
If it's all the same to you.

In January of 1973, the year after my father died and I had left Claiborne, I was a lost soul. Only two months prior, I was at the Keeneland November Sale where scores of people would come up and say, "How're you doing, Arthur? Good to see you, buddy." They'd all pat me on the back with big smiles on their faces.

I was in a position to let people breed to Round Table, Nijinsky, Sir Ivor and all those great Claiborne stallions. Nobody could get to them without an okay from either me or Seth. We were the toast of the sale.

All kinds of people came up saying, "Arthur, we want to help you and Seth any way we can and we're behind you boys."

Yet here it was two months later back at the Keeneland January Sale and the people were as cold and dark as the weather. I knew I would be seeing a lot of those same people, and I needed their comforting greetings and warm wishes. But most of them wouldn't even give me the time of day.

It was uncanny how their demeanor had changed toward me, and it was one of the toughest lessons of my life. I was now a nonentity, a nobody.

Now I was the guy who, for all they figured and what the rumors were, had just given up and walked out on his heritage. Benjamin Franklin said it best, "Now I have a sheep and a cow, everybody bids me good morrow."

I had no sheep. I had no cow. Hardly anyone bid me good morrow. One of the few people who was kind to me was Ted Bassett, the President of Keeneland. He put his hand on my shoulder and said, "You'll do just fine, Arthur. All will be well."

For several years after I left Claiborne, people would call me Seth. I would have to tell them I was the "other brother". The great Bold Ruler, the sire of Secretariat, had a brother whose name was Independence, and I would tell them that was me.

I had gone from living in a lovely four-columned mansion to living in a four-room cottage. I had to borrow twenty-five thousand dollars from Sullivan just to keep going.

I did get a substantial inheritance a couple of years later and I started borrowing against it and buying cheap mares and all the good surrounding land anyone would sell me. I was going to be a land baron—spelled b-a-r-r-e-n. I eventually bought eighteen farms consisting of 4,600 acres of prime Bourbon County land making me one of Kentucky's largest landowners.

When I finally bragged to him years later about being bigger than Claiborne, Handsome Sam Ransom put our new status in the proper perspective. "Well, Boss, we may be big in size but Claiborne's big otherwise."

In buying all of that land, I was only trying to position myself for luck to run over me—and eventually it did.

In 1976, Bold Forbes won the Kentucky Derby and then on pure courage won the Belmont. Aaron Jones, a new client of mine from Oregon, bought him for $4 million cash.

I was going to syndicate him into thirty-six shares, at $125,000 each and stand him at Stone Farm for $25,000. It would be my first big stallion deal.

I told Mr. Jones that I knew several people I thought would take a share, but most of them didn't. The breeders wouldn't support Bold Forbes. I was in trouble. I had even gone over to Newmarket, England for the December Sale, and I couldn't sell any shares there either.

I had guaranteed to do this, and now it looked like I couldn't. I was on the hook for almost four million dollars.

I came back to the farm in despair. I remember one night in January. It was ten below zero. I had an old dog, Hobo, and he had cancer and was dying. He was in there by the fire and the wind was howling and I was chain-smoking cigarettes thinking, "Well, I'm a failure. I'm ruined, what am I going to do?"

I humbly asked God to please help me. I thought, *I can't even syndicate a good stallion. I'll end up broke and disgraced. The advisors must have been right.*

Three or four days later, it was up to five degrees above zero and Bunker Hunt, the Texas oil tycoon for whom Seth and I had syndicated Bold Reasoning, called me on the phone. He and I had become friends when I was at Claiborne, and he asked how the syndication of Bold Forbes was going. He had talked about maybe taking a couple of shares.

I told him frankly the syndication was not going well at all and that a lot of competing stallion farms were going around town knocking Bold Forbes. Bunker was his own man and he paid them no heed. He said, "What if I take a third of the shares in Bold Forbes?"

I said, "Oh my God, that would be the most wonderful thing. I feel certain he will make a good stallion."

Bunker took twelve of the thirty-six shares, and Warner Jones took one and helped me sell a couple more. When C.V. Whitney took two, we were off and running.

That was one of the best things anybody ever did for me. I might not be a failure after all. I got Bold Forbes syndicated, and he went on to become a good stallion siring a Kentucky Oaks winner.

I had taken a big bite and tried to make my mark. Bunker Hunt had saved me. For that I will be eternally grateful. Still, those freezing winter nights were filled with fear, especially that one particular night when the wind was howling, and the chill factor was twenty-five degrees below zero.

If you've never been in that position, it is hard to imagine. I just figured I was doomed and that I'd be the laughingstock of the industry.

At the time I thought maybe I had good reasons to get drunk. I was up on my little farm and my brother was running Claiborne and was the king of the horse industry, having just syndicated Secretariat. I had a lot of self-pity and self-recrimination, so when the opportunity to anesthetize myself presented itself, I would take it. I would get drunk.

One time, I was out with a girl and we both had too much to drink. I didn't want to drive because about six months earlier I'd been put in jail for being asleep in my car in Lexington after I had been drinking.

She was driving and this was our second or third date and I said, "I love you."

She said, "I love you, too."

I said, "Let's go to the Continental Inn."

And she said, "All right, let's do."

And I said to myself, *"Oh man, here we go."*

About that time, we heard the siren.

"Oh shit."

The cops pulled her over. One came up to the car and said, "Young lady, have you had anything to drink?"

She answered, "Just a couple." The officer made her get out of the car and walk the line. She was wobbly, so he told her to wait in the back of the squad car. I asked where he was taking her, and he said, "To jail."

"Oh, please don't do that," I said. "I asked her to drive and it's my fault. She's from a nice family. She's got a respectable mother and daddy. Look, sir, if you were in Ireland or somewhere, you'd be nice and just let us go home."

"You ain't in Ireland, buddy. You're in Kentucky," he said. "She's goin' to jail."

When I started walking away, he said, "Where the hell you think you're goin'?" And then he came around the car and got in my face.

"I'm gonna get somebody to come get me," I said.

He said, "No you ain't. You're goin' to jail, too. Public drunkenness. Stay right where you're at."

I had no choice. The paddy wagon came for her, and I was sitting in the back of the police car on the way to jail with two officers. "Listen to me, please," I said, "This is really going to hurt me and my family. We've got Secretariat on our farm and if you take me to jail, it will be bad for Claiborne, bad for me, bad for the horse industry and bad for Kentucky."

Then the officer in the passenger seat turned around and said, "You own Secretariat?"

I thought they were about to let me loose, and I said, "Yes, sir, he's at our farm."

Smirking, he said, "Well, by God, you tell us where he's at and we'll go get him and put him in there with you."

They threw me in a big cell with seven other guys. I was mad as hell because I hadn't even been driving, and we had been thwarted from going to the Continental Inn for the night. One of the drunks was mouthing off and I finally told him to shut the hell up.

He said, "The fun don't even begin till I get to your mother."

I knocked him halfway across the cell. The rest of the drunks cheered. Then the cops came in and handcuffed me to a pole. The last thing I remember before going to sleep on the floor was the guy rubbing his jaw and saying, "Man, this motherfucker shoulda been a prize fighter."

After the mandatory four hours were up, I called Sullivan, and he got me out about two o'clock in the morning.

A few years later, the police caught one of my friends, Albert Yank, for drunk driving when he was in town for the yearling sales. For his one call, he told them he wanted to phone his friend Arthur Hancock to come and get him out of jail. One of the cops said, "Arthur Hancock? That's the wildest sonofabitch we ever had in this jail. You wanna go see Secretariat?"

One day after the races at Saratoga, I was having a drink as usual, this time in the company of a wiser, older man. This was 1975, three years after Daddy died so I was thirty-two. Buggs was about seventy-five or eighty, and for years had been the maître d' at The Reading Room.

I said, "Buggs, do you think I'll do all right in life? Will I be able to do anything worthwhile?"

Nodding toward my glass of bourbon, he said, "Oh yeah, you'll do all right as long as that stuff don't get you. I've seen a lot of promising young men like you over the years come and go through these doors only to go to hell."

That really hit me. That was the first inkling that I might really have a problem. Buggs was a wise old sage and I said to myself, "I should heed his words." But, admitting that to myself would not be easy. I still had a long way to go.

LONELY LONELY LONELY ME

Lonely, lonely, lonely me
I'm as lonely as any man can be
Without you I'm not me, and soon I'll cease to be
Lonely, lonely, lonely me

The days have passed the weeks have gone
For eight months now I've been alone
They say time will erase, but more time I just can't face
Lonely, lonely, lonely me

Each night before I fall asleep
I cling to my pillow and I weep
Where are you little girl, how could life be so cruel
Lonely, lonely, lonely me
Lonely, lonely, lonely me

CHAPTER 12

Staci and Arthur

I WAS ON A merry-go-round and couldn't get off. I would drink hard every couple of weeks. I had girlfriends from Paris, Kentucky to Paris, France, in Ireland and England, but there was no one special. Life seemed hollow and lonesome.

That summer, I was at the Keeneland July Sale and went by Warner Jones's Hermitage Farm Consignment to look at a couple of horses for a client. As I was standing there talking to Mr. Jones, I looked out onto the show-ring and a beautiful blonde girl was showing one of his horses.

I said, "Mr. Jones, who is that girl out there showing that horse?"

He looked sternly at me and in his deep, authoritative voice said, "Her name is Staci Worthington, and you leave her alone . . . she's a nice girl!"

During that sale, Staci had seen me walking around the barn lot several times and asked her good friend, Nancy Cloud, who I was. Nancy said, "That's Arthur Hancock. Watch out for him. He's the wild, black sheep of the family. He likes fast cars, fast women, and bourbon whiskey."

Later that year at the November Breeding Stock Sale at Keeneland, Staci was again working for Mr. Warner. The local paper had snapped a photo of her going in to the ring with a mare. I was looking at another horse when I saw her. Having seen the picture in the paper a few days before, I stopped her to try and make conversation and commented on the nice picture. We exchanged pleasantries and that was that.

The following year, Keeneland was hosting a Summer Sales dinner party. I had run into Staci that afternoon at Mr. Warner's barn and asked her if she would like to go with me. She thanked me but said she already had plans to go. I saw her there with her date that night and spoke with her for a few minutes. She was a college coed, eleven years younger than me and, even though I was attracted to her, I rationalized that the age difference and my rather wild lifestyle probably precluded any type of relationship from developing.

In April of 1977, I was going to have dinner with Paul and we met at Nelly Kelly's. The service was very slow, and when the waitress didn't even bring us a glass of water, I said, "Let's get the hell out of this place." We were about two blocks from the Library Lounge, which was also a popular restaurant and bar near the University of Kentucky campus and I suggested we go there.

About a week before, I had been very lonely and depressed one evening and was having serious thoughts about what in the hell was going to become of me. I was thirty-four years old, living on my small farm in a little house by myself, and even though the business was picking up for me, I had no meaningful relationship other than a roster of casual girlfriends. I seriously prayed to God, "Father, if you can hear me, please send me someone."

After graduating from UK with a degree in equine marketing, Staci had taken a side job as a waitress while she looked for gainful employment in the horse business. She had worked lunch shifts at the Library over the last few months but had never worked a single dinner. That afternoon, a coworker asked Staci if she would cover the dinner shift for her. It was that very same night that Paul and I came in and sat down. As fate would have it, we were seated at one of the tables in Staci's section. She said that when she saw us, she thought to herself, "Oh no, not him . . ."

We had a very nice dinner, and, at some point, I asked Staci about her plans for the summer and if she would like to come to Stone Farm to help us get the yearlings ready for the summer sale. She gave me her number, said she would think about it, and to give her a call in a couple of days. When I did, she agreed to come and help us.

I loved Sam Ransom. When I left Claiborne, he came with me. Sam was some kind of a shaman as well as a genius at rhyme and comedy. He had all kinds of sayings, a lot like today's rappers but long before their time. He used to joke that he was Flip Wilson's father. While he was in the army he got to dance with Shirley Temple when she visited his base. He was one of a kind!

If I was down, I'd talk to Sam and the clouds would lift. He was always cheerful and upbeat, and being around him was like a breath of fresh air. He was a philosopher and had a way of putting things that always made sense. He was a pillar of positivity.

If a horse lost a race, Sam had a positive answer: "Last one got away, next one's got to pay."

When a horse won a race, Sam would say, "He ran so fast he shit in his own face."

He had a big smile, which would light up the darkest of days. When I'd talk to him about death, he'd say not to worry, that the being who numbered the grains of sand on the beach, the stars in the sky, and the hairs on your head, also numbered your days on earth. "When it's your time, it's your time."

Sam always laced everything with humor. I told him one day that I had tickets for us to fly to New York to see Tap Shoes run. He said, "I don't know about gettin' on that plane, Boss."

I said, "Sam, you've told me over and over that when it's your time, it's your time."

Sam looked at me and said, "That's true, but it might be somebody else's time on that plane, and I'd be on there with him."

With my "main man" Handsome Sam Ransom, "the women's pet and the men's regret"
– Hancock Family Photo

On Staci's very first day at the farm, Sam said, "Miss Staci, the boss likes you."

She said, "Well, Sam, I'm dating someone."

Sam was always ready with an answer. "Why you want to fool around with a claimin' hoss when you might could have Bold Ruler his-self!"

Over the next two months, I saw Staci every day at the farm as we worked getting the yearlings prepped for the upcoming sale. Sam never missed an opportunity to let me know he could tell that she liked me. Given his uncanny and perceptive ability, I believed him. Sam turned out to be our matchmaker!

Staci and I shared a few lunch breaks together, but our first real date was on the Fourth of July. Rudy and Peggy Bicknell, good friends of mine in Wilmore, Kentucky, had asked a few of us to come over to play tennis and have a cookout. We all had a good time and, late in the afternoon, right before we were going to cook the steaks, Rudy suggested that we take a ride on his motorcycles and motor scooters.

I took one of the motorcycles and Staci rode one of the scooters. We were all going out through a big open field when I began to ride the motorcycle in circles around Staci, who was riding the slower scooter. I said surely that thing will go faster than that. As she took the challenge and gunned the throttle, I remember looking back over my shoulder just in time to see her front wheel go down into an unseen groundhog hole, flinging her through the air right over the top of the scooter.

She landed flat on her face in a cow pile, and I rushed over to see how she was. It was not good. Her arm was hurting and there was a lot of blood in her mouth. I got the car and took her to the emergency room at Central Baptist Hospital in Lexington.

The place was a nightmare. Two people came in who had been shot, and they brought another man in on a stretcher who gasped several times and then died from a heart attack right in front of us. Finally, they were able to see her.

They X-rayed Staci's wrist, which was fractured, and they had to clean out and stitch up the inside of her mouth. To say the least, it was not a first date which boded well for the future. While driving her to her apartment from the hospital, I said, "Damn, you're tough. I think I'll just have to marry you."

With a fractured wrist and twenty-five stitches in her mouth, she couldn't help the farm anymore with the yearlings.

We saw each other often through July and August and then, after the September Sale, we decided that we would take a break for a few weeks, just to see how we felt about one another. A wise old man once told me that you should never marry somebody unless you feel like you can't live without them.

When I was dating Staci, I had a client named Roy Bowen, who was very successful in the shoe business and a warm and wonderful man. He was quite a character, often with a wild streak like myself, and over the years he became a dear friend.

He first introduced himself to me over the phone. He kept calling, wanting me to write a song on the phone with him called *Dropout* based on the hook, "*I dropped out of school, when you dropped out of my life, and I dropped out of your heart.*" He said I ought to like it because I had dropped out of Claiborne. I think he admired me and wanted to help me.

Roy regularly came to Lexington for the horse sales. We had dinner one night where he met Staci, and the next day he said, "I'm going to tell you something, young man. You ought to marry that girl—you need to marry that girl!"

I said, "Roy, I'm not ready to get married. I'm only thirty-four."

He said, "Young man. You're a dear friend of mine, but you're no bargain; you better marry that girl."

It got me to thinking . . . maybe I am no bargain.

A few years later, Roy and I ended up naming a horse *You're No Bargain*. He made sixty starts and won over $400,000 for us!

My mother never liked any of the women I considered marrying. After I dated Mamie from Nashville for nearly four years, Daddy was already looking for a house for us on Claiborne when Mama talked him out it.

Mamie had graduated from Harpeth Hall, an upscale girl's prep school. She was blonde, beautiful, and an outstanding student at Vanderbilt. When she would visit me at Claiborne, she was shy, reserved, and perhaps a bit intimidated. Every time I mentioned her, Mama would say in her deep southern accent, "Ahhthuh, you need someone who can entuhtain and tawk to people if you'ah gonna be in the hoss business."

After Mamie and I broke up, I got engaged to a Catholic girl from Louisville but whenever her name came up, Mama would start jabbering in Latin and making the sign of the cross, like a priest giving a blessing. Then she would imitate a screaming baby. This ultimately psyched me out and I remained single.

When Maria came from Germany to visit a family in Lexington, I thought I was in love again. Mama didn't like her either, because she was German, and Mama had lost friends in the war.

The first time my mother met Staci was when I brought her to the big party Claiborne always had before the Keeneland July Sale. There was a gourmet dinner in a large tent with a top dance band from New York. It was a joint affair with an international guest list generally described as "everybody who is anybody in the horse business." We had a nice time and right before we left,

Staci thanked Mama for the party, and told her how nice it was to meet her.

The next day, Mama invited me down to have lunch. She pointedly asked, "Who was that goil you brought to pahty with you last night?"

When I said her name was Staci Worthington from Louisville, she replied, "What does her fathah do?" I told her that he was a well-known and highly respected dentist.

She said, "Well, she didn't even have the decency to thank me for the pahty."

But she had, I said, and had done so profusely, and I suggested to Mama that she had been too busy to remember it.

"I beg to diffah," she said.

I knew right off by the weird stone-cold look on her face what had happened. She was quite intuitive, and I think she sensed that Staci was special to me.

By the end of September, Staci was working for the Rogers at Idle Hour Farm, helping break their yearlings. They say that absence makes the heart grow fonder and that seems to have been true in both our cases. I remembered what the old man had told me about never marrying unless I found someone I thought I just couldn't live without. I felt that way about Staci. When I stopped by Idle Hour one morning and asked her to marry me, she said yes.

I went to Louisville and met with her father, Dr. Worthington, and asked for his approval. He jokingly told me she must see something in me he didn't, but if that's what she wanted to do, it was fine with him.

It just so happened at the time that my mother was taking a cruise in the Orient with some of her lifelong friends and they wouldn't be back until the end of October. I knew if I didn't go ahead with the wedding that Mama would talk me out of it. Her father, Seth Walker, was known as one of the most persuasive and respected lawyers in the South. She was just like him when it came to talking—charming and convincing.

Staci had lost her mother suddenly a few years earlier and didn't want to plan a wedding without her. So, rather than wait around, we just decided to elope to Nashville where I had been born, gone to school, and had a lot of friends. Paul came down to be my best man, and Staci's childhood friend Anne stood up for her. We got married in a small ceremony at my friend Bill Shwab's house. Afterward, the wedding party went over to the Belle Meade Country Club, where my mother's sister, Aunt Katie had invited us for a lovely dinner.

I had not had a drink all that summer because I had gone on a six-month pledge. Problems with alcohol were beginning to pop up and I was beginning to realize that I couldn't handle it like normal people. Staci had never seen me drink.

Aunt Katie had ordered bottles of the finest champagne and wine, and everybody was drinking and toasting. It was a festive evening with close friends and my new bride. When they began to give toasts, I felt that I should, too. So, I had a big glass of champagne and was off to the races again.

I got drunk on my wedding night!

When we arrived back at Shwab's house for an after-party, I got the guitar and started playing some very off-color, dirty songs I had written. Everybody was laughing and having a big time, but I remember looking over at Staci who was sitting there watching me. She seemed to be in shock. She had never seen me like this. The respectable, kind, and considerate Dr. Jekyll had suddenly turned into Mr. Hyde.

The only honeymoon we took was to fly down the next day to watch the University of Kentucky play Georgia. Dr. Worthington picked us up in his plane and I fought a headache and remorse all the way Athens. Then it was back to Stone Farm and back to work.

After news of the marriage had spread around Lexington, friends and acquaintances were making substantial bets as to how long it would last. Their estimates ranged from three weeks to three months to a year. They all lost their bets, and most of them are still amazed to this day that we ever made it.

A week after the wedding, Fred was on his way to Los Angeles when he ran into my mother in the Nashville airport coming back home from her trip abroad. Fred always told the story of her saying to him, "Can you believe it? Ahhthuh gettin' married while I was in the Oh-ri-ent!"

Together after all these years – Bert Morgan Photo

On a Saturday afternoon, in the fall of 1978, I got a call from Mama asking me to come to Claiborne to help her entertain Prince Phillip who was in Lexington on a Royal tour. She was in a panic because Seth didn't want to. So, Staci and I dutifully went down and helped give Prince Phillip a tour of the Claiborne stallions.

At the stallion show, a wonderful man named Clay Arnold, who was a head stallion groom and a salt-of-the-earth person, pulled out a Brownie camera and said "Sir, all the girls in the office would really like to have a picture of you."

"They shan't have it I assuah you," he said.

Maybe he was having a bad day, but this thoroughly enraged me. I kept my mouth shut and didn't say a word. After looking at the stallions, we all retired to Claiborne House for mint juleps in the library around the fire. I drank down the juleps and the Prince left, but I was just getting started. My only outlet was to get drunk and find friends in low places.

From Claiborne, Staci and I went to the wedding of one of her sorority sisters at the little church at Mt. Horeb, an event of which I have little recollection, but that Staci remembers vividly.

We sat with the Theta housemother, Mom Gum, who noticed I was a bit tipsy. At the reception I made a scene, so Staci herded me out the door and to the car to go home. On the way, I insisted on stopping at a rundown bar on Winchester Road for one more drink. By this time, Staci was aggravated and said she would just wait in the car thinking that might speed my departure and we could go home. An hour later, she marched in the bar to find me laughing and drinking with my new best friends. When she couldn't get me to leave, she went out to find a pay phone to call my mother and sister for reinforcements.

I remember Staci returning to the bar and telling me that they were outside waiting. Then she escorted me to the car, and we all went back to Paris. That was not the only time she had to find me and drag me out of a watering hole.

A year or so later, Sullivan and I went to Lexington and had dinner. I was driving a little white Alpha Romeo convertible that I had given Staci as a present after our first child Walker was born.

Paul and I spent the time drinking and talking about the Revolutionary War and the War of 1812. I told him about my father showing me a tree where two English officers had been hanged during the Revolutionary War for the crime of paying the Indians for the scalps of settlers—men, women, and children. We finished off dinner with another bottle of wine.

I left and was on the way home when I stopped at a red light and heard some good music coming from inside a biker bar. I decided to risk going in and having a couple more drinks. When I sat down at the bar, a huge guy with a beard, who had seen my car, came up to me and said he was going to buy the Alpha Romeo and that I was not going to leave until I sold it to him. I did some quick thinking and told him it belonged to my little brother, but if I could get his name and number, I'd have my brother call him.

During this conversation my fight or flight instincts had taken over and I downed a couple of more double shots of Maker's Mark and water. Then I went to the payphone and called Staci, told her where I was, and that there might be trouble. By this time, it was around eleven o'clock. She put our baby daughter, Walker, in the car and came all the way to Lexington, marched into the biker bar, and ordered, "Let's go home." If she hadn't done that there is no telling what might've happened, because it was getting rowdier and rougher by the minute.

Forty-seven years and six children later, we are still happily married. Warner Jones saw me at Keeneland once with Staci and the kids in tow and turned to me and said, "Goddamn, you're lucky!"

I have often wondered what my life would have been like if Paul and I hadn't decided to switch restaurants and go to the Library Lounge for dinner that night. And I have thought 1,000 times about my prayer to God and then that fateful life-changing encounter only a week later. They say that destiny turns on a dime. But something puts the dime in the right place at the right time.

PART

FIVE

CHAPTER 13

Gato Del Sol

ON ONE OF THE luckiest days of my life, I got a phone call from a man I didn't know but who had been told to call me by his trainer, Tom Pratt. He asked me if I would be interested in standing my first stallion, a horse my father had bred named Cabin.

"He will be the leading stud in the wuld . . . we will kill 'em! . . . I am lucky as well as talented and smaht," said Leone Peters in his New York accent.

I liked him right away.

Indeed, he was talented and smart, being the chairman of the board of Cushman and Wakefield, one of the largest real estate companies in the country.

Mr. Peters told me to get ready to board some mares to be bred to Cabin, and, true to his word, before long we had about twenty new mares on the farm.

Cabin didn't do so well as a stallion, but he was the beginning of a long and friendly relationship with Mr. Leone Peters. Together, we had sizable profits, racing success, and a lot of fun.

The first one we bred together, Tap Shoes, was a very good horse. He was bred on a foal share: Mr. Peters owned the mare and I put up a season to the stallion Riva Ridge. He was quite a good two-year-old and won the Sanford and the Hopeful Stakes at Saratoga. After he won the Flamingo Stakes as a three-year-old in 1981, we sold a half interest in him to my mother and Horatio Luro, the trainer of Northern Dancer, for a very good price.

With Staci at the Flamingo Ball the night before the big win by Tap Shoes in the 1981 Flamingo Stakes at Hialeah – Bert Morgan Photo

Tap Shoes went off at 9/2 as one of the favorites in the 1981 Kentucky Derby, and I was devastated when he finished only tenth. I figured I'd probably never get another chance to win the race that had so obsessed my father.

Strathcona, a mare I owned in partnership with Mr. Peters, had a daughter named Dunfermline who won the St. Leger in England. Of course, that made the mare worth a lot of money, and couple of days after the race, I took a call in my office and a voice said, "Hello, Lord Porchester here, calling for Her Majesty the Queen."

I thought it was somebody playing a prank and started to hang up, but I didn't. Instead, I said, "Yes, sir, Lord Porchester," and he replied, "Yes, Her Majesty is quite keen to purchase Strathcona."

I couldn't believe the Queen of England wanted to buy a mare from me. I told him it was an honor and that I would certainly sell her, if not give her to the Queen, but that I had to check with my partner, Mr. Peters.

I had been so taken aback with the call that I had failed to ask how much the Queen wanted to pay. That was of course the first thing Mr. Peters wanted to know. When I returned the call, Lord Portchester told me the price was £25,000.

I called Mr. Peters and told him what Her Majesty was offering. He said, "What the f- - - ? Tell the Queen she can go shit in her hat."

When I called Lord Porchester back, after three layers of receptionists, I heard him say, "Poatchestah hyahh." Without mentioning the Queen's hat, I said we were very sorry, because it would be an honor, but that my partner does not wish to sell.

Mr. Peters and I owned another horse named Leonato that was going to run in a big stakes race in England and we decided to go over there. I went to New York and had dinner with him at a great Italian restaurant and the next morning he sent his chauffeur to pick me up in a long black Mercedes limousine and we drove to Kennedy International.

To get into the Royal Enclosure at Ascot, we had to have vouchers from the State Department. We had applied for them, but they hadn't arrived in time. So, even though we had on our morning suits and top hats, we had no credentials to get into the exclusive area.

At the gate of entry, a very tall and stately gentleman said, "Sir, I'm terribly sorry, but you can't come in without a pass."

Mr. Peters, a man of great charm, shook hands with the gentleman, winked and said, "Here's my pass," and with that, put a hundred-pound note in the stately gentleman's hand and patted him on the back.

"Right this way, suh," he said with a twinkle in his blue eyes.

The Queen's Jubilee was in progress, and I had never seen such pageantry. There were trumpets playing, banners flying, and exquisite coaches pulled by white horses carrying the Queen and Prince Philip down the racetrack.

Then they played the English national anthem, which is the same melody as "My Country, 'Tis of Thee". I had goosebumps and tears in my eyes. Mr. Peters nudged me in the side and said, "Pompous cocksuckahs."

We had another very good horse together named Hawaiian Sound that I bred, and we owned with Robert Sangster, an English friend of mine and a top international breeder. The horse was second in the English Derby and was now running in the prestigious Benson and Hedges Gold Cup. He won!

When they got to the Winner's Enclosure, Mr. Peters told Robert, "You get all the trophies. I'm getting this one." Then he went up on stage for the presentation. There were two beautiful English girls and a lord who presented the trophy. While the staid old gentleman was giving a little talk about the race, Mr. Peters pinched one of the girls and she said, smiling, "Now, now, Mistuh Petuhs."

Then the gentleman told Mr. Peters, "I am so proud to present you with the traditional and cherished Benson and Hedges Gold

Cup." He opened a case and handed Mr. Peters a small gold trophy about six inches tall.

Mr. Peters took one look at it and said, "This thing? This is all I get?"

There was a low murmur from the crowd. The next day the newspapers were not very complimentary, one of them even saying, "*The Ugly American has arrived in England.*"

But that was Mr. Peters. He was larger than life. His word was his bond. No matter what happened, he would always tell you exactly what he thought. And he was right about the trophy being small. He didn't even want it and gave it to me. But I was proud of it and was happy to accept it.

When we first met, he told me what he really wanted to do was to win the Belmont Stakes since it was held near his hometown of New York City. And together, we bred the winner! Risen Star was arguably the best racehorse Secretariat ever sired.

Risen Star was bred, foaled, and raised on Stone Farm. He came back out of Louisiana to Kentucky and ended up beating Claiborne's great horse Forty Niner in the Lexington Stakes at Keeneland. Then, he finished fourth in the Kentucky Derby and might have won if he hadn't been trapped behind horses. Mr. Peters told me that he was so happy to have the luck and success that we did.

Risen Star went on to win both the Preakness and the Belmont, just as Mr. Peters had dreamed. By a tragic quirk of fate, he died a week before the Belmont victory.

Mr. Peters had been right. He was very lucky indeed, and so was I to have known him.

I bought Peacefully at Saratoga as a yearling for $20,000 and Mr. Peters went in as my partner. We bred her to Cougar, a stallion I stood at the farm who was an outcross from Chile. The idea was that he might be the kind with the "hybrid vigor" my father had talked about.

The first foal we got was a filly named Tasha Two who didn't show much on the track but proved to be a good broodmare. The second year, we got a colt who was so small that when he was born, I made the comment, "This little sonofabitch will never amount to a quarter."

But Handsome Sam Ransom kept saying time and again as the little colt grew up, "Boss, this is the Derby hoss."

Sam was a great judge of racehorses. As a boy, he had galloped Count Fleet for John D. Hertz, the rental car czar from Chicago, over on the Stoner Creek Farm near Claiborne. Sam liked the colt's long stride so much that he talked my father into going to see him.

Mr. Hertz had him for sale for $15,000 but when Daddy saw him and said he'd take him at that price, Mr. Hertz, who was very smart, said, "Bull, if you like him that much, I think I'll just keep him."

Count Fleet ended up winning the Triple Crown in 1943, the same year I was born. Sam also singled out Risen Star for a great future and we sold him against Sam's advice.

Mr. Peters and I tried to sell the Peacefully colt, too, in the Keeneland July Yearling Sale, but they rejected him. Since Sam thought he was going to win the Derby, we decided to just keep him and race him. And thank God we did, because he went on to validate—in spectacular style—not only Daddy's hybrid vigor theory but also the horse wizardry of Handsome Sam.

How the horse got his name is a big part of the story. There was a gray cat at the barn that would sit out in the sun, and just that image, so peaceful, no worries, with his eyes half-closed, was a kind of meditative pleasure to see. I still carry with me the vignette of that cat relaxing in the sun.

Gato Del Sol's sire, Cougar, was known as "The Big Cat" and his dam was Peacefully. That's where we got the name. We tried to register it in English—Cat of the Sun—but we couldn't so we got it in Spanish.

We sent Gato to trainer Eddie Gregson on the southern California circuit. At two, he won the Del Mar Futurity from so far back that you wouldn't have given him a chance, but he came on and won it by a head. We ran him in the San Felipe and the Santa Anita Derby as a three-year-old, but he didn't place. Then he was second in The Bluegrass Stakes at Keeneland. In all three races he was closing at the end just like he did at Del Mar.

Gato Del Sol was clearly a product of Daddy's breeding philosophy that outcrossing often produces a superior performer, a theory he had learned while crossbreeding fruit flies in a Princeton genetics class. Years later, however, when asked to speak at my twenty-fifth Vanderbilt reunion, I was able to tell my classmates that it also had something to do with a lesson in geometry.

Which horse gets which post position in the starting gate is decided by drawing numbers from a pill box. At the draw for the 1982 Derby, Gato Del Sol drew post twenty-one. I was devastated. No horse had ever won from a post position past number fourteen in the previous 107 years of the world's greatest race!

The conventional wisdom had always been that the horse in the outside post has to run so many feet farther to the finish line than the horse in post position one, which is up against the rail. This disadvantage is offset in races run by humans on a circular track by staggered starting blocks, which ensures that each contestant travels the same distance.

The disadvantage to a horse that draws the outside post in a twenty-one-horse Derby field on the track at Churchill Downs is magnified by how long it takes him to move closer to the rail before he reaches the first turn.

When I got home from the draw, I thought about how many times my father had failed to win. He had five contenders over the years and all of them for one reason or another didn't get to run or had something freaky happen in the race.

There had to be a curse on the Hancocks. Too bad, too bad. We have no chance, I thought. I collapsed on my bed. A little bird was singing on a limb right outside my open window and I remember thinking, "You're supposed to be good luck, but you can't help us now, little birdie."

And then I began to wonder why it was considered so bad to be all the way out there? A vague recollection of some right-angle triangle geometrical theory occurred to me, but I could not remember the formula. I called Sullivan. His nickname was the "math whiz" in school. He scored in the ninety-ninth percentile on the National Merit Scholarship tests.

"Oh, that's the Pythagorean theorem," he mused. He explained that we had the base and the height and that we were looking for the hypotenuse, which is the square root of half the base squared plus the height squared. "Let me get my calculator . . ."

The line went quiet as he did the calculation. Then he asked me how much distance I thought we would lose by being that far out in the gate. I said ten to fifteen lengths, which is about eighty to one hundred and twenty feet. But I had no idea.

"You know how much you lose?" he asked.

I said, "What, twenty lengths? I don't know."

Paul said, "A little over two feet."

I said, "What?"

He said, "A little over two feet. That's all! Let me refigure this bastard."

So, he did, and it was a little over two feet. He was really excited. "Now, Hawk, that is if you go in a straight line. If you come in too quickly, you'll lose a lot of ground because you will be moving sideways while the others are going forward."

I was ecstatic. I jumped up off the bed and went over to the window. The little bluebird hadn't moved and kept right on singing. "Maybe we're not beat after all!"

It was all about keeping the horse outside long enough and, since he came off the pace anyway, there was no need at all to come rushing into the rail.

Yeah, yeah! So, I called Eddie Gregson, who had been cum laude at Stanford. I could tell he was really down.

"Nobody gives us any shot," he said, "It's the worst damn luck I've ever had drawing way out there."

I said, "Well, how much do you think we lose, Eddie?"

He said, "I don't know, but whatever it is, it's insurmountable."

I said, "I'm going to tell you how much we lose." And I told him the whole story about the triangle.

"Oh my God, Arthur," he said. "You've got to be kidding me. It can't be."

I said it can be. It is.

Then Eddie Gregson excitedly said, "I'm calling Eddie."

He meant our jockey Eddie Delahoussaye, who called me back elated. Quoting Paul, I told him the trick was not to come to the rail too quickly.

I said, "Just put the end of that stretch between the horse's ears, like you would the muffler of a tractor on a distant tree when you're plowing ground down there in Louisiana."

The weird thing about the 1982 Derby was that all the better horses were temporarily sidelined and missed the race for one reason or another. You can call it chance or coincidence. I don't know. But I believe it was something out of the ordinary that I can't explain.

In 1974, I bought 180 acres right across the road from the original Stone Farm, owned by a man named Reuben Pribble. Mr. Pribble had been on a navy vessel in Pearl Harbor the morning of the Japanese bombing. He had seen most of his friends killed and it was said that it was a miracle that he escaped alive. He was a very intelligent man, and I thought the world of him even though he seemed a bit eccentric like many brilliant folks. He told me that the farm was haunted.

I hadn't owned the farm very long before I began to wonder if what he told me wasn't the truth. There was a pond that would hold water for a month or two, go dry, and then a month later do the same thing again.

There was also a cistern near where an old house had once stood. Mr. Pribble's wife, Mary, swore to me she once saw a man come up out of the cistern, walk around the barn, and then go back into it and disappear underground. Later, our night watchman told me he had seen what appeared to be car lights in the barn, but when he went to check he found nothing. I didn't believe him and told him to call me the next time he saw them.

Sure enough, he called, and I went over and saw what looked like car lights glaring at us. He refused to go with me, but I went to check, certain I would find a car or truck inside. But the barn was empty. That was when I first began to think about selling the farm.

That was just the first of many strange occurrences there. There was a big oak tree on the farm and on the side of it could be seen the face of a man. Everybody who saw it was astonished. And once when I was under another tree, trimming branches, a big limb fell out of the top and struck my head so solidly I was knocked to my knees.

There was another big dead tree that I set on fire and when the bark fell off, clearly carved in the side of the tree was the name *Sharonne*

Belle 1872. I couldn't help but notice the old French spelling and to this day I have often wondered whether she was a relative of the legendary *Bell Witch*, who was said to have haunted a farm in Robertson County, Tennessee earlier in that same century.

One day, we saw a rooster hanging by the neck from the front of the top of the tobacco barn. He had somehow become entangled in some twine. That barn later mysteriously burned down in the middle of the day for reasons we never knew.

Then the eeriest thing of all happened. One day while I was mowing, a large whirlwind began to move across the field. A crow was floating on the top of the funnel, spreading its wings, and riding the wind across the field. I had never seen anything like it in my life and couldn't help but wonder if it wasn't some sort of an omen.

I mentioned this to my friend, Fred Foster, who was very attuned to the spiritual and the supernatural. He called his Cherokee Indian friend, Minnie, whose grandparents had been on the Trail of Tears from North Carolina to Oklahoma in the 1830s. He said she was a shaman and he asked her about this strange phenomenon. I couldn't wait to see what she said, although I was a bit skeptical.

Minnie said what I had seen was a very rare and spiritual occurrence. She told him it was a sign that my dreams would come true, and that good fortune would befall me. He told her my dream was to win the Kentucky Derby and she said it would happen!

Black cats have always been bad luck to me. The last time I crossed one's path was in 1988. I was walking on a farm road and the fields were muddy. I thought to hell with it, it's just a superstition, and I crossed its path. The next morning, Staci was carrying our baby daughter Lynn down to the kitchen, slipped on the stairs and broke her ankle. Her foot was turned all the way around like the head of the girl in the movie *The Exorcist.* When the doctor at the hospital told her he had to reset the bone, he knew the procedure would be so painful that he gave her a stick to bite down on. Then he twisted her foot forward. She didn't even utter a whimper.

Maybe the reason black cats are bad luck for some people is because they serve as a warning. In 1981, when we had Tap Shoes on the Kentucky Derby trail, we were rushing up to Keeneland for the Blue Grass Stakes where he was the favorite when a black cat ran across the road.

We were trying to get to the track in time for lunch. I said, "Screw the damn cat, we gotta get to Lexington." When we arrived, a strange looking cloud, only about four miles in diameter, settled over Keeneland. Right before the race, it rained two inches in just thirty minutes. We had to scratch. Tap Shoes hated the slop and couldn't stand up in the mud. The black cat had struck!

Tap Shoes had also been jinxed the day before the Derby when Mr. Peters said, "How do you get to the winner's circle?"

I said, "Mr. Peters, that is tempting fate."

He retorted, "Fuck fate! I want to know how to get to the winner's circle!"

Tap Shoes might very well have won if the thick rubber band Mr. Luro used to tie his tongue hadn't broken as he was being saddled right before the race. In its place, Mr. Luro had to use a cloth tongue-tie which made Tap Shoes mad and intractable.

More eerie than that, five days after the Derby Mr. Peters lost his best mare, the dam of Tap Shoes. Bold Ballet and her foal, a full sister to Tap Shoes, were both struck and killed by a lightning bolt from a sudden spring storm that passed over the farm. As Shakespeare said in Hamlet, "There are more things in heaven and earth, Horatio, than are dreamt of in your philosophy."

The very next year in 1982, we were in the Derby again with Gato Del Sol. We were coming back to Paris from a dinner in Lexington when Staci saw a black cat cross in front of us. She yelled, "Stop!"

I screeched to a halt, and we waited for a car to cross his path and break the spell. None did, so I just backed up and went down through a tunnel that came out on the Winchester Road. On the other side, here came a cop, lights flashing. He pulled me over and asked for my driver's license.

I asked politely what I had done. He said, "You went up a one-way street."

I said, "Sir, I know you've heard a lot of stories but let me explain to you why I did it."

Then I told him about Tap Shoes and the black cat and that our horse, Gato Del Sol, was running in the Derby on Saturday. I said, "A black cat just crossed our path, and I can't chance it again."

He said, "Here's your license back, Mr. Hancock; good luck Saturday. I don't blame you."

About ten days before the Derby at a meeting of the Kentucky Racing Commission, Anita Madden, the wife of my friend Preston Madden, and the hostess for many years of the most famous Derby party in Lexington, came rushing up to me in a clearly urgent manner.

"Arthur, I've seen it," she said. "I've seen it."

I wondered what in the world was on her mind and asked her what she had seen. She said she'd had a vivid dream that I was going to win the Kentucky Derby. She'd had these premonitions before, she said, and they had always come true. It gave me chills.

One key to winning the Kentucky Derby is the horse must be able to get the mile and a quarter. That last eighth of a mile separates the men from the boys. Gato was bred to get a mile and a half, so I was hopeful he could go the distance. But you never know.

At the regular Tuesday night Derby Trainers' Dinner, four days before the race, I ran into the great jockey Bill Shoemaker, who was riding the number eight horse Star Gallant.

I asked him if he thought Gato had any chance on Saturday. He said, "You're gonna win the motherfucker." Just like that.

I excitedly asked why he thought so, and he said, "'Cause you're the only horse in the race that can get a mile and a quarter."

That was the first time I really thought we had a shot. When Bill Shoemaker spoke about horses, you listened!

With the great Bill Shoemaker – Hancock Family Photo

When Gato came out of the gate on Derby day, Eddie did exactly as he was told. I remember my hands were shaking holding my binoculars when I heard somebody behind me say, "Why don't that gray horse get on in there!"

Eddie was way wide, and he finally drifted in somewhere after an eighth of a mile, running behind some pretty wild fractions being set by Cupecoy's Joy, who went six furlongs in 1:10 and change. But that kind of pace was what a closer like Gato needed. He was dead last all the way around and then he began to pick off horses. When he came flying around that final turn, Adger was hitting me on the back, yelling, "He's coming . . . he's coming. It's all over but the shoutin'! It's all over but the shoutin'!"

He was coming and he took the lead. It was over. Fred was in our box that day. He yelled, "Arthur, Arthur, Minnie was right!"

I didn't believe it was real until they put his number up on the tote board. It seemed surreal, like a living dream. I was afraid somebody would take it away from me. That's the way I felt; that some way, somehow, winning the Kentucky Derby couldn't be possible. It was too good to be true, but it was!

Then, they made it official. Gato paid forty-four dollars for a two dollar win ticket. For the only time in my life, I felt like I could literally walk on air. Have you ever dreamed that you were flying? I had dreamed it but now it was real. I felt I could just float right up in the air. It was truly an out-of-body experience.

Walt Disney said, "All our dreams can come true, if we have the courage to pursue them." My dream came true that magical afternoon.

Staci and I were so excited that we went down the wrong steps and got lost in the crowds going to the Winner's Circle. The National Guard was surrounding it, standing as a blockade with their guns across their chests. They were all over six feet tall.

Gato Del Sol winning the 1982 Kentucky Derby – The Tony Leonard Collection

They saw Staci and me running across the track from the wrong direction and when we reached the winner's circle, one of them said, "Buddy, you can't come in here. This is for owners."

I said, "Sir, I need to get in; I own the Derby winner."

He said, "Sure you do, buddy, and I own Churchill Downs. Now get the hell outta here."

About that time Governor John Y. Brown saw us and kept motioning for us to come through. I said, "Look, the governor is waving us in!"

"Well, I'll be a sonofabitch—go right on, buddy!"

While we made it just in time for the presentation, the delay with the guardsman made us late for the win picture.

During the trophy presentation, I credited my good fortune to the horsemanship I had learned from my father. I said, "I'd like to dedicate this Derby to my dad who taught me everything I know about how to get here."

I thought, I'm out here in the winner's circle; I've left Claiborne, and now I'm the first Hancock to ever win the Kentucky Derby!

A dream come true in 1982 – Bert Morgan Photo

When we left the Winner's Circle, we all went to the Director's Room at Churchill Downs. The celebration was on! There was every kind of Kentucky bourbon whiskey imaginable lined up on a shelf and in true Kentucky tradition we all got into it. Celebrities and well-wishers came by to congratulate us. There was total euphoria and happiness.

One of our guests, a newcomer to the game, my friend Tom Tatham from Houston, had bet $10,000 to win on Gato at twenty-one to one. Lynn Stone, the CEO of Churchill Downs had Tom's $210,000 delivered to the Director's Room in a garbage bag. I had bet $500 based on the Pythagorean theorem and so had Sullivan, who would rarely bet over two dollars. My pal Adger had wagered a thousand, as did Fred.

With my partner Leone Peters in the Churchill Downs Directors Room after we won the 1982 Kentucky Derby – Hancock Family Photo

They finally closed the celebration about nine o'clock. Lynn Stone and the rest of the Churchill executives had just as good a time as we did. They said it was the longest celebration after the Derby they had ever hosted at Churchill Downs and one that they would always remember. They were extremely nice and accommodating and bid us a warm farewell.

We had a small bus to take us back to Lexington and someone from Churchill arranged for a police car to follow us to the city limits of Louisville to make sure we didn't get robbed. That bus was rocking, and Tatham suggested that we pull off the interstate and ride through a small town throwing out hundred-dollar bills, but we decided that might be bad publicity.

Staci had arranged a win or lose dinner in the Men's Grill at Idle Hour Country Club at eight o'clock, but we didn't arrive until eleven. The staff was still patiently waiting for us when we poured out of that bus whooping it up like rodeo cowboys.

Robert, the maitre d' at Idle Hour, had been there for thirty years. I had known him since I was eight years old, and we were very fond of one another. Everybody at the club knew and loved Robert like a member of the family. When we all bounced euphorically off the bus, Robert and his staff were there to greet us.

Ten days before, after the Blue Grass Stakes at Keeneland when Gato had run second, Staci and I went to Idle Hour to have dinner. We saw Robert and I gave him a big hug and a hundred dollars and said, "Robert, the little boy has come up with a good horse for the Kentucky Derby. For good luck and good karma, bet this on Gato in the Derby."

So, I expected him to be floating on air. But he just stood there frowning and staring at the ground. I looked at him, apologized for us being late, and said, "Robert, what in the world is the matter?"

He shook his head forlornly.

I said, "Oh my God, Robert, don't tell me you didn't bet that hundred dollars!"

He looked sadly from the ground and into my eyes, still shaking his head.

I said, "Robert, why didn't you bet?"

"Your brother told me to save my money." he replied.

We remedied that situation immediately when people started pulling out hundred-dollar bills and stuffing them into Robert's breast pocket. I had never seen a man's demeanor change so fast in my life.

Robert was not the only friend who had benefitted from crossing the path of Gato Del Sol. The policeman who let me go for driving up the one-way street, Steve Racz, bet his entire paycheck on Gato, netting him several thousand dollars. I still talk with him from time to time, and we once appeared on the popular Caywood Ledford radio talk show together to share our story.

A few days after the Derby, I received a very nice letter from Mr. Phipps. He congratulated me and told me how proud my father would have been. The letter brought tears to my eyes, and I replied with a nice note of appreciation.

About the tenth time Sam Ransom had told me, "This is the Derby hoss," I said, "Sam, if this horse wins the Kentucky Derby, I will get you a brand-new car." A few days after the race when things had settled down a bit, Sam came into my office.

I said, "Sam, I know why you're here. I have seen some nice Oldsmobiles, Buicks and Chevrolets."

He looked at me wistfully and replied, "Boss, all I ever wanted was a Cadillac or a Lincoln."

I said, "Sam, if it hadn't been for your intuition, we would've sold the horse, so you go and pick out any car you like and drive it home. Thank you so much, Sam."

He got himself a brand-new Lincoln Continental and when he drove it to the farm and showed it to me, we both had tears in our eyes as he gave me a big hug and thanked me. Sam kept the car until he passed away, and his wife later told me with a smile that Sam loved that car more than her!

I remember one night in one of our philosophical discussions when I was very stressed and worried and quoted John Milton, "The mind is its own place, and in itself can make a heaven of hell, a hell of heaven."

Sam's reply was, "That's true, Boss. Your mind can come up with a lot of shit, and that's all it is—shit. That's just the devil talkin'."

Sam was with me at Stone Farm for over twenty-five years. One night Sam came out and went fishing in the pond by our house. He caught a big mess of bass and headed home about dark. He died that night in his sleep. He was 75 years old. Sam was unique, one of the most remarkable people I have ever known. He was a wonderful blessing, an uplifting presence in my life.

When Gato Del Sol retired from the racetrack, we brought him home to Stone Farm to stand at stud. He didn't have much success so when we received an offer from Germany to buy him, we accepted. He didn't make it as a stallion there either. After Staci heard that American champion Exceller had ended up in a slaughterhouse in Europe, we repurchased Gato and brought him home to Stone Farm where he lived happily ever after. He was the toast of the farm and visitors would come to see him from around the world.

Staci and Gato del Sol – Barbara Livingston Photo

Buried in our yard – Bobby Shiflet, Frames on Main

He lived out his days in a lovely, lush paddock. Staci visited him every day and brought him carrots and peppermints. He also loved an occasional beer. And when he passed on, we buried him in our yard, evoking comments from friends that "you must really be a redneck to bury your Kentucky Derby winner in your own back yard!"

And Anita Madden's vision had come to pass. She was certainly a seer, and after Gato had won, she told me that I would win the Derby again someday.

CHAPTER 14

Arthur "B" for Backgammon

BACK IN 1978, there was a funny movie called *Every Which Way but Loose* that produced two hit songs for country singer, Mel Tillis, who was in the movie. One was called *Coca-Cola Cowboy* for no reason that made any sense. But it had a line in it I can't forget. "You've got an Eastwood smile and Robert Redford hair . . . And you taught me how to say I just don't care."

Now every time I hear the name of that movie or the line in that song, I can't help but think of John Y. Brown Jr.

I had known John Y. since we were both young men. We were casual friends and I had once stayed at his house in Louisville when he was married to his first wife Ellie. My father had known his father, who was a good lawyer and a congressman from Kentucky.

Being ten years older, there is no doubt that John Y. knew about my story of fistfights, automobile accidents, alcohol excess, and dropping out of Claiborne.

I knew him mainly as a hero of the business world who had married Miss America, Phyllis George, and made a fortune building Kentucky Fried Chicken into a global company. Then he became the fifty-fifth governor of the Commonwealth of Kentucky. The mere wave of his hand had gotten Staci and me admitted into the Derby Winner's Circle at Churchill Downs.

The morning after the Derby, a state-owned helicopter landed on the lawn at Stone Farm. Governor Brown had called and invited Staci and me to accompany him to the annual Kentucky Colonel's Barbecue, a venerable political speaking tradition that for twenty-five years was held on the first Sunday in May, the same weekend as the Kentucky Derby. Governor Brown and the First Lady of Kentucky, Phyllis George, were already on board, as well as the comedian Foster Brooks.

What looked to me to be the entire Kentucky State Police force was waiting for us when we landed on the grounds of Wickland Mansion near Bardstown, Kentucky. It was the site of Federal Hill, the plantation that inspired Stephen Foster's *My Old Kentucky Home*, about eighty miles south of Lexington. The mansion had served as the home of three previous Kentucky governors.

State troopers lined our path through the cordoned-off crowd of people yelling and trying to get a close-up view of Governor Brown and his beautiful wife. It was as though we were with the king and the queen, reliving a medieval dream.

Following his political speech, the popular Governor Brown singled us out on the stage and told the story of my leaving Claiborne and losing my birthright, only to start Stone Farm with just a few leased acres and "just yesterday winning the Kentucky Derby."

John Y. introduced me and gave me a nod to say a few words. It was the first public speech I had ever given. There were several thousand people there, all happy and waving their arms and shouting. I kept it short. I said, "I'm proud to have won the Kentucky Derby, but I'm even prouder to be a Kentuckian!" The crowd went berserk—hollering, screaming and raising their beer mugs. John Y. gave me a big smile and hearty thumbs-up.

From the barbecue, the helicopter took us to Cave Hill, John Y.'s estate on the outskirts of Lexington for the governor's big after Derby party. As the Kentucky Derby winning guest of honor, I heard myself being announced to the glittering crowd as a Horatio Alger story. I gave my second speech of the day telling all of those celebrities how I had just lived my lifetime dream. At one point, I found myself standing in a circle with Governor Brown, Arkansas Governor Bill Clinton, and my illustrious cousin, John Jay Hooker Jr., a close friend of the Kennedys who had twice run for governor of Tennessee and whose goal at the time was to become a member of the United States Senate. I didn't realize then that all three of them had the talent and the ambition to become President of the United States.

With John Y. Brown signing autographs at the Kentucky Colonel's Barbecue – Hancock Family Photo

When one of those gorgeous starlets walked by, we all quit talking and just stared. Then, John Jay said, "My, my, my, would you look at that!"

And Bill Clinton said, "Get in line, John Jay. Get in line."

John Y. had treated Staci and me like royalty, and I felt as though I had a new friend who really cared about me. He said, "Those who used to laugh are no longer laughing, Arthur. You have pulled off the unimaginable."

At some point during that weekend, John Y., whose vast experience as a high-stakes gambler in both recreation and business qualified him in the minds of many as a professional, asked me if I ever played backgammon, which I had.

I had played only with amateurs for ten dollars a game and had already learned that gambling was not my strong suit. After once losing $500 on a race, I rarely ever even bet on my own horses. But I must have been intoxicated from the euphoria of winning the Derby because I boastfully answered the governor's question by suggesting that the middle initial "B" in my name stood for backgammon—Arthur "B for Backgammon" Hancock. When he was told of that remark later, Fred said, "Arthur, you and I should write a song entitled *The Original Fool*."

When I got another call from John Y. a few weeks later, he said that he and Phyllis were free from obligations that evening and would like to stop by the farm so we could find out if the "B" in my middle name really stood for backgammon.

Staci fixed dinner and that night the governor's long black limousine escorted by a highway patrol car pulled up in front of our little farmhouse. I called Staci over to the window to share my amazement at the scene—the governor of Kentucky showing up at our house for dinner! I thought to myself, winning the Kentucky Derby had landed us in high cotton.

This was seven years before I finally quit drinking, so I was still prone to my old habits of getting drunk whenever I had something to celebrate or regret. We started out with wine at dinner and worked our way up to Jack Daniels as we pulled out the backgammon board and started the game. I can still hear the *bluke-bluke-bluke* sounds of doubles leaving the mouth of the bottle into my glass as we played game after game on into the night. Staci and Phyllis had fallen asleep on the couch talking about the children. It must have been around one in the morning when the highway patrol escort returned. I didn't even remember the Browns leaving.

On the morning after the backgammon game, I realized just how intoxicated I had been the night before and that I had lost heavily, maybe as much as $10,000, but I just didn't know. When I talked to John Y. that afternoon about the amount, he said he had my signed IOU for $375,000!

I was stunned. It was like a punch in the gut. I had no recollection of ever signing an IOU.

The 1982 Derby purse was a record $522,000. The winner's share was $417,600, but I only owned half the horse, so it had to be split with Mr. Peters, the co-owner. As badly as I needed the money, I had just lost all of my earnings and more and was now deeper in debt than ever.

Worse, I had lost it in a drunken stupor to my friend. But he was a gambler, and I was a drunk. Once again, my enemy alcohol had laid me low. And the path I had to choose to pay my debt to the governor would lead me right into the middle of the federal grand jury investigation into the infamous *Bluegrass Conspiracy*.

I had known Wendell Lee "Sonny" Rawls Jr. as a Chattanooga prep school graduate in my class at Vanderbilt in the early 1960s. Nearly twenty years later, early in 1983, he showed up in Kentucky and suggested that we have dinner. At the time, he was a reporter for the *New York Times* and had already won a Pulitzer Prize for investigative journalism.

Over dinner at Vanhoose's Steak House, Sonny casually mentioned that there were rumors of "big trouble brewing in the Bluegrass." He said that a federal grand jury investigation was underway into a conspiracy based in Kentucky to smuggle and sell cocaine and illegal guns all over North and South America.

Then he dropped what one journalist has since told me was a "bomb" question that was most likely the purpose of his visit. "Do you know someone named Paul Sullivan?"

I said, yes, that he was my best friend. Then Rawls told me that Paul's name had popped up in the investigation that was still sealed and secret at the time. Shocked, I simply could not believe what I had just heard.

When I told Paul, I thought he was going to have a heart attack. He had not heard a word about it, even though he was a well-connected and highly respected lawyer in a top Lexington firm.

Sullivan's cool demeanor and smooth way of handling things while we were growing up had earned him the nickname "Silky". In the mid-1950s, there was a Thoroughbred racehorse named Silky Sullivan, famous for running from so far behind that no one believed he could win, but he usually did.

For the first time since I had known him, Paul was no longer "Silky". He was understandably a nervous wreck over the possibility that his sterling reputation and the brilliant career he had worked so hard to establish might be in jeopardy. He had no idea that it had anything to do with his friendship with Arthur "B for Backgammon" Hancock.

It was not long before two FBI agents showed up at my farm office and began asking strange questions about why I had gone on some mysterious raft trip down a river in West Virginia with a Frenchman, a veterinarian, and two prominent Kentucky horsemen—a breeder and a farm manager.

I knew the men who went on the trip, but I had not gone. I asked the FBI men what happened that made them interrogate me about it. They said they could not discuss the investigation. One, a tall dark-haired, scary-looking guy, said, "Mr. Hancock, you should know that lying to the FBI is a crime punishable by imprisonment."

I repeated that I had not gone on the trip. And he reminded me a second time that lying to the FBI could land me in federal prison for seven years. Then one of them said, "Mr. Hancock, we know you went on that raft trip."

I said, "For the last time, I did not go on any raft trip."

They left me without a doubt that they didn't believe me.

By this time, having heard that there had been heavy cocaine use on that raft trip, Paul and I had a good idea what all this might be about. It looked very much as though my crazy night of backgammon had produced an even crazier sequel. At one stage it required me to ask Paul to run an innocent errand on my behalf.

And the visit with the FBI convinced Paul's law firm that the only thing for me to do to help Paul was to tell the complete backgammon story to the U.S. Attorneys in charge of the *Bluegrass Conspiracy* investigation.

I was ready to face a firing squad for Paul if necessary. After all I had seen him accomplish and all he had done for me since we were teenagers, I was going to stand up for him, no matter what. He had worked his way through college and furthered his education via the Air Force. Then he had worked his way through law school. That his family name and his career might be destroyed by something I had done was unimaginable.

So, I knew what I had to do. Accompanied by one of the lawyers in Paul's law firm, I went to see Bob Trevy and Louis DeFalaise, the two U.S. Attorneys for the Eastern District of Kentucky and told them the full, bizzare story of the backgammon game.

At first, I had challenged John Y. Brown's claim that I had lost $375,000 in the backgammon games. I could not possibly have lost that much money playing what I considered a friendly board game, not unlike a night of playing Monopoly with house guests. But John Y. insisted we were playing for real money and when he showed me the IOU I had signed, I knew I had been too drunk to remember it.

After some negotiating help from people who knew John Y. better than I did, the governor cut the debt in half to $187,500. I pleaded with him to reduce it to $50,000 but to no avail. I honorably agreed to pay it back over time in small increments and deliver the payments to Jimmy Lambert, a Lexington nightclub owner and mutual friend who had been a classmate of John Y. at the University of Kentucky.

Everybody including the FBI knew that Lambert and Brown were close friends. But the day I had asked Paul to do me a favor and drop off my cash payment at Lambert's house, neither of us had any idea that Lambert was one of the suspected leaders of an infamous illegal cocaine ring and that his house was under constant FBI surveillance.

Most of my early payments to John Y. had been in small amounts, but I had been busy with the farm and had accumulated $75,000, which I had tried unsuccessfully all day to deliver myself to Lambert's house in Lexington. Rather than take it back to Paris, I went by Paul's law firm and asked him to drop it off at Lambert's for me.

Lambert was not at home that night but his business partner, Phil Block, accepted my payment from Paul in front of a female witness, who turned out to be working in the Lambert household as an under-cover agent of the FBI. Paul's favor to me ended up in an affidavit as part of the evidence in the allegations against Lambert and Block, both of whom eventually went to prison on cocaine charges.

Paul was on the brink of losing everything because he had delivered my cash to a house that was under FBI surveillance. After hearing my story, U.S. Attorney DeFalaise turned to Trevy and said, "Bob, that story is so unbelievable, it has got to be true."

That totally exonerated Paul, but it all could have ended very differently. Neither Paul's name nor mine was ever publicly mentioned in connection with the *Bluegrass Conspiracy*.

With my lifelong friend Paul Sullivan – Hancock Family Photo

CHAPTER 15

Royal Hangover

"OH MY GOD, the Queen is coming to my mother's house for lunch and Mama wants me to sit beside her!"

I couldn't believe it. I remember the first time I flew to England and getting goosebumps when I looked out the window and saw English soil. As a student of history, I recalled the exploits of the knights and the warriors over the years. Now, the head of it all, Her Majesty the Queen of England was going to be sitting right beside me. She was coming to Central Kentucky to tour the bluegrass farms because of her deep love for Thoroughbred horses.

On the eve of her visit, Sullivan and some of my friends and I went down to Vanhoose's Steakhouse in Paris and began to drink whiskey. We had a big time celebrating the Queen's visit—and boy did I feel bad the next morning! I had a terrible headache, a sore throat, and felt like there was some sort of a cold or allergy coming on, so around ten o'clock I took a couple of antihistamines to mitigate the severity of my symptoms.

Staci and I went to Claiborne House about eleven forty-five to await the arrival of Her Majesty at noon. The secret service was there along with the Kentucky State Police. There was even an agent with a missile in his truck that could shoot down a helicopter or plane if need be. The tension and excitement were palpable.

The Queen and her entourage arrived in high spirits and were very courteous and friendly. You don't shake hands with the Queen. You nod your head and say, "Nice to meet you, Ma'am." Thereafter, you address her as Ma'am. We all went into the library, and everyone had a drink before lunch. I was so nervous I ordered a double bourbon on the rocks, which I soon wished I had never done.

With Queen Elizabeth and all the Queen's Men inspecting our stallions at Stone Farm
- The Tony Leonard Collection

After cocktails, we all filed into the dining room. Mama was seated at one end of the long table and the Queen at the other. Seth was on her right and I was on her left. My hands were shaking, exacerbated by the two antihistamines and the amount of whiskey I'd had the night before—not to mention the double bourbon I had just downed.

As soon as we were seated, the Queen began talking to Seth about some of the stallions at Claiborne. I was very glad she didn't look at me right away because I was indeed a mess. I had broken out in a profuse, cold sweat and I could even feel it dripping from under my arms. I happened to look down the table and the Queen's lady-in-waiting occasionally glanced disdainfully at me. She knew something was amiss.

When Nathan brought in the vichyssoise, the Queen was still talking to Seth. I picked up my soup spoon, and my hand was trembling terribly. I almost dropped it. Now the lady-in-waiting was watching me intently and giving me those mortified glances that only the English can give. I tried to take a spoonful but had to put it down because my hand was shaking so badly that the vichyssoise was flying from the spoon. That's when two beads of sweat dropped off the end of my nose right into the bowl.

I thought I was going to have to excuse myself and, in a last-ditch effort to prevent a horribly embarrassing situation, I gulped down my julep cup of ice water, wiped my face and the top of my head and neck with the napkin—and prayed that the Queen would not look my way. About that time, one of the maids refilled my julep cup and I downed that as well in three gulps.

Thank God. No sooner than the shakes and the sweats had come on they departed, just as the Queen looked my way and began to inquire about a couple of the stallions that I stood at Stone Farm. She was extremely knowledgeable about horses, and after a few minutes chatting with her, I found her to be genuine and down to earth—just like some of my neighbors in Bourbon County.

She knew about the horse I had bred named Hawaiian Sound who was only beaten a nose in the English Derby. We spoke about him as well as Gato Del Sol. I told her a few stories about that, and she seemed quite appreciative and entertained. The luncheon was a success and a once in a lifetime experience.

After lunch, the Queen honored us with her presence at Stone Farm to see our stallions. And when she left, she was kind enough to say that she had very much enjoyed my stories and hoped to see me again sometime. To this day, I remain ever thankful that she didn't look at me the first few minutes of that unforgettable luncheon.

Staci hosting Queen Elizabeth during her visit to Stone Farm in 1984 – The Tony Leonard Collection

KING ALCOHOL

See the wreckage he has caused, the long unending road.
The sad destruction in his wake, as subjects bear his load.
Shattered hearts and families, relations torn asunder.
Faith and love all ripped to shreds, as the King rides on like thunder.

Asylums, morgues, and funeral homes are where he holds his court.
His subjects moan in misery as the King enjoys his sport.
Broken homes and suicides, scenes that are surreal.
Shootings, beatings, and drownings are cards he likes to deal.

Still folks don't blame King Alcohol for the troubles they endure.
They blame their plight on other things and feel that he's the cure.
One would think they'd refuse to live such wretched lives,
But they think he's their closest friend—and that's how he survives.

His subjects cringe at just the thought of life without their master.
And wade for him through thick and thin, which brings to them disaster.
They call on him incessantly with hopes he'll make them well,
But what they think will be the cure—turns into living hell.

Cunning, baffling, powerful, he waits quite patiently.
Night and day he's on his throne, while they're out on a spree.
But, oh, when morning sheds its light on the cold and heartless day,
His subjects shiver from the plight the King has brought their way.

Hospitals, jails, disputes and lies, wretched unhappiness,
This merry-go-round of grief and woe, brings tragedy and death.
And paying his toll as best they can while living out their lives,
These shivering denizens of his realm, come to their demise.

Few escape his tyranny, his patient, poisonous sting,
Though some succeed in their escape and find a greater King.
A subject asks who is this King, and wherein may I find him?
The answer is this simple truth—It's God, as you define Him.

I have come to believe that my problems with alcohol came not from the Hancocks, but rather from a chemical intolerance inherited from my mother's father, legendary Tennessee lawyer Seth McKinney Walker Jr.

Jack Norman Sr., a nationally known Nashville lawyer, regarded my grandfather Seth as a role model. He paid tribute to him in a newspaper column in 1989, calling him "the most effective advocate I have ever had the opportunity to observe. As a contemporary, I have never known stronger character, greater professionalism, or a more beautiful personality. A fierce adversary, he was yet always courteous and gentlemanly in his advocacy."

My father witnessed his in-law's legal skills firsthand when a Claiborne syndicate was having some trouble completing an agreement to import the great stallion Nasrullah from Ireland to stand in Kentucky beginning with the 1951 season.

The $350,000 purchase from Irish breeder Joe McGrath was perhaps my father's crowning achievement. It was similar to what his father had done in the 1920s by importing Sir Gallahad III from the French. Daddy had negotiated the deal on behalf of a syndicate that included some of the best breeders in America—his own father and William Woodward, John Hertz, Harry Guggenheim, two members of the Phipps family, Marion Dupont Scott, George D. Widener, and several others.

But as the time for Nasrullah's import neared, it became clear that he would likely be named the leading English/Irish sire of 1951. The bottom dropped out of the British pound, the currency in which the original agreement had been structured, and McGrath began showing signs he might be backing away from the deal.

So, not long before his death, my grandfather Seth accompanied my father to Ireland to try and seal the deal. Family lore has it that it was his courtroom skills at explaining to McGrath how reneging on a deal would negatively affect McGrath's and Ireland's sterling reputation among America's horsemen and captains of industry. He told McGrath over a few toddies that people in America had a saying that an Irishman always keeps his word.

His efforts turned out to be very successful. Nasrullah was fully syndicated and the speed that he infused into American bloodstock became a major factor in its rise to the top of the Thoroughbred breeding industry over the next fifty years.

Unfortunately, my Grandfather Walker's love for Jack Daniel's whiskey and his relationship with its founder, Lem Motlow, is also legendary. Big Seth—as we called him—was an alcoholic who died at the age of fifty-eight.

He had apparently met Motlow when both were members of the Tennessee House of Representatives where my grandfather at just age twenty-seven had been speaker in 1919–21. And, in 1936, at the height of my grandfather's career, Motlow hired him as defense lawyer when he was charged in St. Louis with murdering an L&N railroad conductor.

The case against Motlow appeared to be strong. He routinely traveled to St. Louis on weekends to attend mule auctions. There was only one witness in the dining car when the shooting occurred. It was a preacher who also rode the train every weekend from his home in one end of St. Louis to his church in the other.

Motlow had ordered a porter to quickly ready his bed for the trip east because he had a headache. But the porter said he was not allowed to do so before the train left the station. When he refused, Motlow threatened him with a loaded pistol that accidentally discharged when the train lurched and killed the conductor who was coming through the door into the car.

My grandfather had a sixth sense that the preacher might be disingenuous in some details of his testimony, so he kept questioning him about how he had been paying his regular train fare each weekend for the past twenty years. At first, the preacher claimed he had a free pass from the railroad. Seth asked to see it, but the preacher said he had forgotten it. Seth asked him to bring it the next day, but he didn't. Under aggressive cross-examination, the preacher finally admitted that he had been using a pass belonging to a member of his church.

My grandfather pulled from his pocket a free L&N pass given to him in his role as general counsel for the railroad and asked the preacher to read aloud instructions on the back that the pass was "Not Transferable."

Then he concluded by saying, "Preacher, you call yourself a man of God. You have come in here and accused this honorable man of a despicable crime, but you are nothing more than a sixty-five-cent thief and you have been robbing the L&N Railroad every day for twenty years!"

The jury found Motlow innocent, and he paid my grandfather with distillery shares, worth two cents each in those days, that eventually amounted to a significant interest in Jack Daniel's Distillery.

It was Seth's habit to celebrate at home for a couple of days with Jack Daniels after he had won a big case. During one such spree, he drove his car over an embankment into a shrub hedge. When the police arrived, he confidently told them that if he hadn't been such a good driver, someone might have been killed!

For the rest of my grandfather's life, the basement of his home on Warner Place in Nashville's elite Belle Meade neighborhood was perpetually filled with case after case of Jack Daniel's whiskey, which he freely handed out to judges, opposing lawyers, and friends at a time when selling liquor by the drink in Tennessee was illegal. And of course, his relatives got their share, too. Many a bottle of Jack Daniel's arrived full and left empty from Claiborne House while he was alive.

My grandfather, legendary Nashville attorney Seth M. Walker – Hancock Family Photo

After he served three years in the Air Force, Paul and I were back in action. We were still running mates and would go out to bars and drink and party. Around 1975, however, my drinking really started getting to him.

One night I jumped up on the roof of his car and then down on the hood. He took a swing at me but missed, hit the car, and broke his hand.

He told me, "You're not the same, Arthur, you're changing."

When I bought 1,542 additional acres for Stone Farm in 1977, Paul closed the sale for me. This was a big deal. I had already bought the property next to it, and the farm across the road and several smaller tracts nearby. This was the seventh farm I'd bought. Every time I'd buy a farm, we'd get drunk. It had become a ritual and tradition. So, that night we went out and got drunk.

Staci and I had only been married a few months. We were still living on the little original 100-acre farm. I didn't go home. I didn't call either. I just got drunk. I slept in the car in Lexington.

The next morning it was raining, and I felt terrible. So, I went over to the Library Lounge at about ten o'clock when they opened, had lunch, and started drinking beer.

Staci found out where I was, left, and went back to Louisville. When I got home that afternoon, she was gone.

Talk about being depressed! I called her father and asked if he minded me coming over and talking to Staci. He said, "No, come on."

She reacted as she typically would to my shenanigans. She was stone cold, calling to mind a line from a great Keith Whitley song, "You say it best when you say nothing at all." The message was clear. She did not intend to tolerate this kind of behavior.

The next time I didn't come home was when I passed out at a friend's house. When I got back the next morning, my bags were packed and sitting on the porch.

Staci's dad had a few problems with alcohol, too, and he took me to my first AA meeting. But I was still far from ready to quit.

One day in 1985, three years after Gato Del Sol won the Derby, I found out that Gato had been injured and could no longer race. On the same day, Staci told me she was pregnant with our fifth child.

That night, Sullivan and I went down to Vanhoose's and got drunk. I got up on stage with the band and sang *Johnny B. Goode*, and a couple of other songs. Mrs. Vanhoose asked me why I drank so much. I told her that I found out that day that my Derby horse was injured and that Staci was pregnant. She told me that her best friend's husband was dying of pancreatic cancer and that she wouldn't even think of drinking the way I did. It put me in my place, and I'll never forget it. She was exactly right. People who drink too much always have an excuse. Either they're celebrating something good or trying to forget about something bad.

When I left there to drive home, the Paris cops were waiting for me, and I spent the night in a jail cell. There was a wino in there who went over and threw up in the sink and then said, "I need a goddamn drink."

I sat there on the bunk with tears coming down my cheeks thinking, "This is it, I've got to quit."

They charged me with DUI. I got out of jail the next morning. Jack McKenzie, my farm manager, picked me up at 5:00 a.m. and took me home where Staci and the children were asleep. I felt awful. I waited until about 8:00 a.m. and called a family friend and recovering alcoholic, John Bell, owner of Jonabell Farm. I had talked to him a year or so before because I knew I was having problems. I said, "I'm ready to go to AA if you'll help me." He said there was a meeting two days later.

I talked to Paul, and he gave me some great advice. "You can beat this charge if you want to . . . but I've seen people who beat these raps and then the next thing comes up, and they'll beat that, and the next thing you know they're just trying to beat everything and end up being a lush or dead in a ditch. Face up to it, Arthur."

Several days later I went to court and the judge said, "How do you plead?"

I said, "I was drunk, your honor. There's no excuse."

The judge seemed surprised by my confession. He looked at me as if he appreciated my honest reply and gave me a minimum fine. I lost my license for thirty days and had to go to driver's school, which was held in Versailles. If I had any doubt about why I was there, on the way to our lunch break, an old man chewing tobacco spat in his spittoon and said to his friend, "Bill, hyar comes them drunks again." That hit home for me.

Over the next few months, John Bell began to take me to meetings, and I felt like I was right where I needed to be. There was just something about the character and good humor of those guys as we stood shoulder to shoulder against our common demon.

It still took me three years and six slips to fully embrace the AA program because like everything else in my life, I had to push it to the limit trying to beat it. I finally gave in to the first step: "We admitted we were powerless over alcohol—that our lives had become unmanageable."

I would go five or six months without a drink and then try it again.

In the meantime, our fifth child, Arthur IV was born. Finally, we had a son after four lovely and healthy daughters. I remember bringing him home from the hospital. We had a big fire going against the February cold and I remember walking up the steps carrying him safely to his crib. As they say in AA, good things happen when you quit drinking.

I eventually learned to distinguish between Dr. Jekyll and Mr. Hyde. I had my last drink in the early morning hours of New Year's Day 1989, just as another good thing was about to happen—Sunday Silence.

PART SIX

CHAPTER 16

Sunday Silence

"YOU'RE GONE, HAWK."

It was 1988 and Sullivan had just finished going over the financials. The horse and real estate markets had both crashed, and I owed about $15 million, which would translate to about $35 million in 2024 values.

What had been worth a dollar was worth thirty cents in 1988 because of a change in the tax laws implemented in Washington. I had borrowed up to my neck to invest in land and more horses than I can remember.

After about two hours of perusing all the information, Paul looked at me gravely and said, "There is no way in the world that you can pull this out with the debt you've got and the current state of the economy."

It literally felt like somebody had hit me in the stomach and a familiar wave of severe depression overcame me. I had a wife and six children. Everything I had worked for looked as though it was going to go up in smoke. I would now be dubbed the idiot the advisors had thought me to be from the start.

Then Paul looked at me with a sarcastic grin and said, "You can always go out to Wyoming or Montana and start Hawk's Bar and Grill and pick that guitar." He thought that was funny, I guess, but my situation was desperate—and I didn't see much humor in it. Paul says he had more confidence in me than I did.

That night, I awoke suddenly in a total panic. It was 2:30 a.m. I knew I wasn't going to get back to sleep, so I got up and went walking across the farm. The night was absolutely beautiful. The stars were all out and the Milky Way was crystal clear. Off in the distance, a fox barked, and fireflies lit up the night. As I walked along, I wondered, "Now, what am I going to do? There's no way out. I have a young family, a mountain of debt, and no answer in sight."

Of all the trials I have been through, this was my most desperate hour. At that time, still in the grip of alcoholism, I found myself praying to the heavens for a miracle. I even gave some thought to driving off the road into a big oak tree. I had a $10 million life insurance policy which would have left Staci and our children financially secure. I tried to rationalize this and remembered my abnormal psychology class at Vanderbilt about what severe stress can do to the human mind. I am not sure I could have ever done such a craven thing, but the thought crossed my mind, if worse came to worst.

I looked toward the heavens and said out loud, "God, please help me if it be your will." I can't describe why, but instantly I had a feeling of absolute certainty that something or someone out there had heard me and that everything was going to be all right. It was an otherworldly experience.

There had been a long stretch in my life where I was skeptical about God. I had been an agnostic, feeling that time and evolution made everything possible. Then one night I saw a mare deliver her foal. Here was a tiny miracle. The mare was nickering and nuzzling her baby. The foal answered her.

I had an epiphany. In that moment, I knew for certain all of this couldn't have simply evolved from a mud hole without a guiding hand.

I thought to myself, "Who are you to say there is no God?" Since that moment, I have come to realize that all of these millions of miracles would be utterly impossible without a higher power. God is either everything or else he is nothing. And I concluded that all of the order and beauty on this earth could not have occurred merely by accident.

The next morning about six, I went to the popular local restaurant in Paris called Louie's, and while I was having a cup of coffee and waiting on my breakfast, I decided to figure up my daily cost of doing business. The prime interest rate in the early eighties bounced around from ten to fifteen percent. I took $15 million times ten percent interest and divided it by 365 to calculate my daily interest expense.

I got the shock of my life. Before even buying breakfast, I started my day with new debt of over four thousand dollars without even counting other farm expenses. I knew that Paul had been right and that I was in big trouble. He had told me that only a miracle could save me. And he was exactly right.

Seth and I had syndicated Bold Reasoning right before I left Claiborne. Later, when I was on my own, I wanted to buy one of his sons and had put together four or five guys to be partners. In 1975, a colt out of a Poker mare came up in the Fasig-Tipton Yearling Sale. But at that time, I wouldn't set foot there because Fasig-Tipton was a rival to Keeneland, and I had just been put on the Keeneland Association Board of Directors.

If I'd have gone over and looked at him, having had a whole year at the racetrack around the dam's sire, Poker, and having syndicated his sire Bold Reasoning, I surely would have bought that colt for what turned out to be a bargain price, $17,000. He turned out to be Seattle Slew, who won the Triple Crown and became worth millions as a stallion. But that fidelity to Keeneland would be paid back to me in spades at the 1987 July Sale when I bought back a gangly son of Halo out of loyalty to his breeder.

Horses like Sunday Silence are rare. Even Daddy never had one like him. I'll never forget driving by the paddock and seeing this little colt with a blaze in his face running in and out and around the other mares and foals. He was silver-gray at the time, like a lot of black horses when they are young. He was doing figure eights, almost seeming to lie down on the ground when he made sharp turns.

He was not the kind of horse Claiborne usually bred. He was neither sired by a classic sire of sires nor from one of the great female families. I would never have bought a horse that was crooked behind. His hocks almost touched—one of those conformation faults Daddy and my grandfather had taught me. But, just as in the case of the ugly duckling, time is a great equalizer.

I didn't breed Sunday Silence, but we raised him at Stone Farm. It was just by the grace of God that I ended up with him. Like the Bible says about the birds in Matthew 6:26—"Consider the birds— do you think they worry about their existence? They don't plant or reap or store up food, yet your heavenly Father provides them each with food."

The breeder of Sunday Silence was my friend and client Tom Tatham, a young Texas oil man who had a passion for racing. Adger introduced me to Tom when he came to the 1981 Keeneland November Sales and bought his first weanling for $500,000. When asked by the press if he was going to get serious in the business, he replied, "This is just an hors d'oeuvre." The filly, named Trezieme, went on to become a graded stakes winner in France and the United States, and was the first horse in the beginning of a long and successful relationship.

With Tom Tatham and John Adger celebrating a big win – Hancock Family Photo

One day, Tom called me and said he was interested in the leading American sire, Halo. I told him I thought it would be difficult to get a season to breed to him, because his book must be full. He said, "Hawk, I think you misunderstand me. I want to buy the horse and stand him at Stone Farm." In a bold move, Tom did just that. In the name of his Oak Cliff Thoroughbreds, he acquired 25 of the 40 shares in Halo and moved him to the farm along with about twenty-five mares. These included a hard-knocking stakes winner with a modest pedigree named Wishing Well.

Three years later, Wishing Well foaled a colt by Halo. Tom's bloodstock advisor, Ted Keefer, absolutely hated this colt from the very beginning. He would come to inspect Tom's stock on the farm and say, "Put that sonofabitch away. I know what he looks like."

Keefer disliked the colt so much it was illogical and sort of spooky—like a voice, or something supernatural trying to tell me something. The colt wasn't all that bad, but every time Ted would come to the farm, he'd always say something negative about him.

One time our farm manager Pete Logan said, "Mr. Keefer, this colt would look mighty good with the roses around his neck." Keefer replied, "The only time that sonofabitch will ever have a rose on him is when he's six feet underground."

I learned something from a story my father used to tell about himself. Miss Disco and her foal were pastured right down in front of the Claiborne office. Daddy looked out there one day and said, "That Miss Disco colt looks like a skinny spider." He told the broodmare manager to take them to the back of the farm because "he's an embarrassment." That foal turned out to be Bold Ruler.

On Thanksgiving morning, 1986, when Sunday Silence was eight months old, he was very ill. He was dehydrated and listless and suffering from a bad case of diarrhea. Carl Morrison, our resident veterinarian at the time, came right over to the barn and began giving him fluids as well as some medicine for his stomach and intestines, but the diarrhea only got worse. By lunchtime, Dr. Morrison had given him about 23 liters of fluids, an enormous amount for a weanling. But the little fella just wouldn't give up.

I had already gone to my mother's house for the family Thanksgiving lunch and expected to get a call any minute that the colt had died. I was surprised when Dr. Morrison called around one thirty. The diarrhea had begun to fade away and the colt's spirits were picking up. Morrison said, "I've never seen a tougher little horse. He just won't give up. It's miraculous."

That fighting spirit was something that stayed in my mind. Whenever Keefer would say something disparaging about him, I would remember the courage the little black colt had shown on that cold Thanksgiving Day.

When Sunday Silence went through the Keeneland Sale as a yearling, I was sitting in the pavilion with my buddy Paul and thinking the colt might bring $40,000 because his mother was a stakes winner, and his sire was Halo. When the bidding stalled at about $10,000, I started bidding and ended up buying him for $17,000, ironically the same price Seattle Slew brought at Fasig-Tipton.

I took the sale ticket to Tatham, and said, "I bought that Wishing Well colt back for you. He went too cheap."

Tom said, "Well, Arthur, we don't want him because Ted doesn't like him."

I nodded, turned away, and stuck the ticket in my shirt pocket. At the time, I owed all those millions, and the thought hit me that I probably just blew another seventeen thousand dollars.

That was the beginning of my ownership of Sunday Silence. Little did I know that he would be the pivotal point of my existence, both spiritually and financially—the miracle that saved me. We were both dark horses that nobody thought had a chance.

Paul went in with me on the horse and we brought him back to the farm and broke him. Paul kept saying he didn't want to race so I agreed to put him in the Barrett's Two-Year-Old Sale in California in hopes we would make a profit.

It was out there when I saw him galloping that I really started to see something in the horse. Jose Cuervos, his exercise rider, told me he would be a nice horse. I talked with Albert Yank, who was the consignor and we decided to put a $50,000 reserve on him. Once again, the colt didn't make his reserve. This time we bought him back for $32,000.

One thing I could never get out of my mind was that unnatural hatred that Ted Keefer had for him. I couldn't understand it and it was like the angels were trying to tell me that, on the contrary, there was something special about the horse.

Then out of the blue I received a call from an agent who said he had a client who would give us the fifty thousand we wanted for the colt. Paul and I agreed to accept his offer. I thought we had a deal and that would be the end of it. Three days later, the agent called and said his client had backed out. So, three times we had tried, and three times we had failed to sell the horse. Eerily, after Sunday Silence won the Kentucky Derby, the agent called again and told me that his client had shockingly committed suicide.

When I got back to Kentucky, I met Paul down at Louie's for breakfast and told him we had no choice but to race the colt nobody wanted. Paul said, no, he wanted out and would take the $16,000 for his half.

I took a Sweet'N Low packet off the table and said, "Paul, if you stay in on this horse, it could be really sweet—but if you get out you could feel really low. Please hang in there with me."

"I don't want to race," he said. "If I stay in, he'll probably break down. If I get out, he'll probably win the Kentucky Derby."

About two weeks later Charlie Whittingham called and wanted to buy in to the horse. I ended up selling half of him to Charlie for $25,000 because $50,000 had been the reserve. When I told Paul that I would like to base his half on the $50,000 instead of $32,000, he said, "No, I sold out at thirty-two." I always admired Paul for that.

A few days after the Barrett's Sale in California, they put Sunday Silence on the van back to Kentucky. Coming through Texas, the driver had a fatal heart attack and the van turned over. While other horses perished in the crash, Sunday Silence miraculously survived and rehabbed in a vet clinic in Oklahoma. When he got back to the farm sometime in April, our vet Carl Morrison called me with terrible news. "This horse is a wobbler." Wobbler syndrome is a spinal condition that renders a horse unable to race. This led me to believe he probably had suffered some nerve damage to his spinal column in the wreck. I went down where he was turned out in a paddock and he was staggering around, uncoordinated behind.

I dreaded telling Charlie, so I didn't call him right away. I was going to, but I wanted to give it some time. About a week later, Dr. Morrison called me and said, "You need to come down and see this Wishing Well colt." None of us could believe it. He was frolicking and bucking in his paddock like nothing had ever happened. It was truly a miracle.

We brought him to the training barn and started galloping him again. He was going so well we sent him back to Charlie in California a month later. After the colt had been with Charlie a while, he called and said he had sold half of his fifty percent ownership to Dr. Ernest Gaillard for $25,000, so Charlie owned a quarter of the horse for nothing.

One morning at seven, the phone rang. It was Charlie.

I said, "What's up Charlie?"

He said, "Just waiting on the help."

It was four in the morning in California, so I knew something was on his mind. He finally got to the point and said, "This big black sonofabitch you've got out here can run a little."

We had about four other horses out there, so I didn't know which one he was talking about.

"Who?" I asked.

"The Wishing Well colt," he said.

That was the very first news I ever heard about the ability of Sunday Silence.

Charlie didn't even remember that we had already named him. A guy named Phil Straw and his family had written letters to several farms offering a list of horse names his wife and children had come up with, and politely asked if we might consider using any of them. We responded and told him that we liked one of them, because it spiritually connected the name of his sire, Halo, and the feeling of serenity of a quaint *wishing well*, which was the name of his dam.

It reminded me of a 1970 Kris Kristofferson song that I loved called *Sunday Morning Coming Down*. So, that is how Sunday Silence got his name. Phil said we were the only farm that had responded to their letter. The name turned out to be magical and we thank Phil and his family to this day.

As I look back on it, without a doubt, Sunday Silence was the gift from God that I had asked for in my hour of need on that beautiful starry night.

After Sunday Silence won the San Felipe as a three-year-old, somebody called and offered me $1 million for a quarter interest. I thought that sounded pretty good and might be worth taking because you never know what's going to happen with horses.

Once again, I called Sullivan and told him about the offer. It didn't take him a second to say that $1 million wouldn't even pay my interest for a year, and that I had better "hold on and hope."

That was some of the best advice anybody ever gave me. Getting the million dollars would've been only a short-term gain but a long-term disaster. For us to survive, we were going to need every dollar Sunday Silence would bring.

Before anyone even knew who Sunday Silence was, I saw Seth at lunch one day at Louie's Restaurant and told him it looked like we had a real nice two-year-old colt that Charlie said "can really run." He asked who it was. I told him it was the Halo-Wishing Well colt.

"Well, that's too bad," he said. "Mr. Phipps has the best horse that he's ever had. It's a damn shame he had to come along in the same year."

He was talking about Easy Goer. And indeed, he would prove to be one of the best Mr. Phipps ever owned.

So, I figured it was going to be the same old thing. The man who pushed me out of Claiborne was going to kick my ass once more . . . just when I was beginning to believe I had a fighting chance.

A lot of strange and positive things—omens to me—happened around Sunday Silence. Even if you weren't superstitious, it would make you wonder.

The Sunday before the Derby, Staci and I took the kids on a picnic on the back of the farm. It was a beautiful day, and we had a wonderful lunch of fried chicken, deviled eggs, slaw, and apple pie. It was a very happy time, even though Staci and I were nervous about running against Easy Goer in six days.

We were all sitting on a blanket when I heard a strange whooshing sound getting louder and louder. I had heard that sound more than once. We all turned around and down in the bottom below the hill saw what was making the noise. About a hundred feet in the air was a whirlwind filled with leaves and small twigs going round and round in a circle.

Omen! A four leaf clover! – Suzie Picou-Oldham Photo

I couldn't help but think of Minnie, the seer. By then, she was in her nineties and living in Oklahoma. Once more, Fred called her and she said the Great Spirit had spoken again, and that whirlwinds would always be good luck for me. Fred would be in the box with us the following Saturday when Sunday Silence and Easy Goer met for the first time in the Run for the Roses.

The Thursday before the Derby, I walked out the back door of the office to go home, terribly stressed about our financial situation. A wild rabbit was sitting less than ten feet away from me. He had a sort of friendly gleam in his eye. He didn't run. He didn't move. He just sat there munching on some clover, looking at me.

For two or three minutes, he stayed right where he was with me watching him and wondering why he didn't run. It was the eeriest thing. I had never seen a rabbit around my office in the fifteen years I had been there. I finally said out loud to the rabbit, "Are you okay?" And he looked wistfully at me then hopped around the bushes and out of sight. I never saw him again.

It was like a scene from *Alice in Wonderland*. I figured that since a rabbit's foot is considered good luck, this had to be a good omen. And even though I was apprehensive that entire week, I got the eerie impression from the rabbit that everything was going to be all right.

As I drove away from the office, I thought of that night Daddy died, when that strange and overwhelming presence had come over me and I had gotten the message, "You go on, bud, and do your best, and I'll see you later."

Among the strangest things about Sunday Silence was the frequent occurrence of the number thirteen. When he sold in the Keeneland Yearling Sale, his hip number was 454, which adds up to thirteen. A year later, when he didn't sell in the Barrett's Two-Year-Old Sale, his number was 313. There are thirteen letters in Sunday Silence, thirteen in Arthur Hancock, and thirteen in the name of his breeder, Thomas P. Tatham.

Charlie Whittingham was born on April 13, 1913, and was seated in row thirteen on the plane when he flew in from California for the Derby. While we were in Louisville during Derby week, Staci and I stayed at the Brown Hotel. They put us on the thirteenth floor.

In America, number thirteen is considered to be unlucky. Watch out, it's Friday the thirteenth! In Italy, lucky thirteen means you hit the jackpot. My father always felt it was unlucky, but it has always been very positive for me.

One morning at Churchill that week, Staci and I met a friend, Harold Black, and we went to the track kitchen for breakfast. Harold promoted music shows and had brought Randy Travis to Stone Farm to see the horses. He later brought Reba McEntire to visit, and I took her to Claiborne to see Secretariat. He came galloping up to us at the gate and Reba said, "Oh my lord, I've got goosebumps all over. Meetin' you, ole boy, is better'n meetin' Haggard the first time."

When we were coming down the kitchen steps, we saw a penny gleaming in the sunlight. I reached down and picked it up. Harold Black said, "Wouldn't it be something if it's dated 1982?"

It *was* indeed a heads up 1982 penny, minted the same year Gato Del Sol had won the Kentucky Derby! We got in, started the car, and the first sound out of the radio was Randy Travis singing "Losing my mind going back in time to *1982*."

On Derby day, two days after finding the penny, Staci and I parked over on the backside of Churchill and walked around the track to the clubhouse with our friends Paul and Lana Sullivan and Tim and Diana Vigors. We were walking along and, just like that penny had jumped out at me, I saw a four-leaf clover growing under the rail of the racetrack.

Tim was an Irishman and a Royal Air Force pilot in World War II and a good friend of my father. He had seen good and bad omens in the war from the Battle of Britain to dogfights with the Japanese over Burma. When he saw me pick up that four-leaf clover, he bet all the money he had with him on Sunday Silence.

The great Charlie Whittingham really liked our horse. Charlie had trained Ack Ack and all kinds of good horses, even winning the Kentucky Derby with Ferdinand in 1986, the same year Sunday Silence was born. But all you heard about the week before the Derby was Easy Goer, Easy Goer, Easy Goer.

When Charlie gave Sunday Silence his final pre-Derby work, I was with him. He went four furlongs in forty-six seconds. It was a little too fast for the sportswriters who kept asking Charlie if it might not compromise him on race day. It concerned me, too, as we walked back to the barn together.

Charlie said, "Arthur, don't worry, we will get the money."

"But all the talk is Easy Goer," I said.

And he turned to me, looked me dead in the eye, and said, "My boy, we will get the money!"

CHAPTER 17

Showdown

KENTUCKY DERBY DAY in 1989 was one of the coldest days I ever saw in May. It was thirty-six degrees and spitting rain and snow under a dark and foreboding sky.

The only thing warm about it was the spirit of Staci and our friends in the box, including the Sullivans, the Vigors, and the Fosters. Without their presence, I probably would have had a nervous breakdown. I tried to cling to that calming encounter with the rabbit, but all day long I had a feeling of gloom and doom. Was I was going to get trounced again by the powerful man who had driven me out of Claiborne?

As they left the gate, I was shaking like a leaf. Everything was on the line. Here I was going up against perhaps the most powerful man in racing. He had ousted me from Claiborne and owned the horse knowledgeable people said was the second coming of Man o' War.

Our jockey, Pat Valenzuela, may have won the Derby in the first hundred yards, sweeping in toward the rail from post number eight and bouncing off the nine horse, Triple Buck, and ending up a length ahead of Easy Goer in the pack.

He ran free of traffic in fourth most of the way around. As the leaders neared the final turn, Valenzuela pulled him off the rail and turned him loose. When he looked back over his shoulder, there was that big red Easy Goer under the great jockey Pat Day right on his hip. Once more, I thought I was doomed, that he would come sweeping past us down the stretch. But here came Sunday Silence again and ran away with it, sideswiping a tiring horse and weaving like a drunk driver all the way all the way down the stretch to the wire. Easy Goer was second. I couldn't believe it.

Sunday Silence winning the 1989 Kentucky Derby – The Tony Leonard Collection

Smiling broadly, the first thing Fred said to me after the race was, "Minnie is a miracle, Arthur. I told you."

I couldn't fathom that we had just won the Kentucky Derby again and that we had beaten the mighty Easy Goer. Then I thought of Paul who was right behind me. We had grown up together as boys and were as close as friends could be. I felt really sorry that he had parted with his share in our Kentucky Derby winner. His advice, counsel, and friendship had been key factors in paving my road to redemption. He looked stunned, and I gave him a hug as we left the box for the Winner's Circle.

It was four months since I had had my last drink. And indeed, something extraordinarily wonderful had just occurred.

Even after our victory, I still feared Easy Goer. I knew the Preakness and the Belmont were coming up and that on a less muddy track, he would again be the favorite. But I comforted myself that at least we'd won the Derby, so it wasn't like everything was riding on the Preakness.

Two weeks later, Staci and I traveled to Baltimore for the next leg of the Triple Crown. In our hotel the morning of the race, we were watching TV when the news came on. The sportscaster said Easy Goer had been picked by ninety-eight of the nation's hundred leading sportswriters to win.

I said to Staci, "Oh my God, these are smart people—ninety-eight sportswriters!" I called Charlie in his room and told him what I had just heard.

He said, "Hell, Arthur, them sumbitches don't even know what color our horse is. Quit worrying, my boy!"

I said, "Well, I'm glad to hear you say that, but they're pretty damn smart, Charlie." Then I changed channels and the very first words from the sportscaster were, "Yes, very few of the experts give the *chestnut* son of Halo any chance of beating Easy Goer today."

Of course—Sunday Silence was black!

Remembering what Charlie had just said to me, I looked at Staci and said, "We're going to win the Preakness."

She agreed absolutely. She said, "If that's not an omen, I don't know what is."

Earlier that morning, we had gone to Pimlico to watch our horse in his final pre-race gallop. And just as Sunday Silence was walking down the path next to a wire fence, an awful noise arose that sounded like a baby screaming. It was spooky. A big gray cat had a black cat pinned up against the fence. He was growling at him, and the black cat was shrieking to high heaven. I remembered the gray cat for whom I had named Gato Del Sol. The omens were unmistakable.

I have never seen a more thrilling race than the Preakness of 1989. Coming into the final turn, as Sunday Silence began to go for the lead, Easy Goer came sweeping around him. It looked as though we were beaten. Deflated, I let my binoculars drop to my chest and bowed my head. "He shut us off." I said to Staci, "It's over."

I was looking down when Staci started screaming, "He's coming back, he's coming back!"

I brought my binoculars up and couldn't believe what I was seeing. Sunday Silence was right back—head to head and eye to eye with Easy Goer. The roar from the crowd was deafening as they fought stride for stride down the stretch to the wire.

We weren't sure who had won, and I wouldn't budge an inch from the box until the official sign was posted. Never tempt fate. It would have been a terrible feeling to have started down only to find that we had run second.

Some say it was the most exciting Preakness of all time. When they made it official, we were absolutely ecstatic, jubilantly celebrating all the way to the Winner's Circle. On our way to the trophy presentation, I heard my friend Alex Campbell, a major shareholder at the bank where I owed so much money, say, "Golly, this could save Arthur!"

After the Preakness, all the Eastern sportswriters were down in the mouth. They had put their professional opinions on the line for

"The Race of the Century" Sunday Silence winning the 1989 Preakness Stakes
— The Tony Leonard Collection

Easy Goer and now they had to eat their words. When they asked me to say something about the race, I couldn't resist, so I quoted these lines from *The Battle-Field* by William Cullen Bryant:

"Truth crushed to Earth shall rise again. The eternal years of God are hers. While error, wounded, writhes in pain and dies among his worshipers."

Mama congratulating me after winning the Preakness, with friends Ted Bassett and Alex Campbell
– Keeneland Library Meadors Collection

At the post-race press conference, a reporter asked me if I didn't feel a bit like comedian Rodney Dangerfield, who always said, "I don't get no respect."

As if on cue, I broke into Aretha Franklin's hit song *Respect*, complete with the "sock it to me" lines. So the Eastern press socked it to me. A *Baltimore Sun* reporter sharply criticized me in an article about the race. He and his cohorts just couldn't stand being so wrong about their darling, Easy Goer. On the plane from Baltimore to Kentucky the next day, I began to write this song:

SUNDAY SILENCE

When all the dreams I dream do not come true
And the friends I have turn out to be so few
When it seems the world is closing in on me
Sunday Silence soothes my soul and sets me free.

Every time things seem to turn around
Something else comes up to get me down
And while I do the best that I can do
Sunday Silence gives me strength to make it through.

Here comes Sunday Silence again
On the track of life sometimes you lose
Sometimes you win
We all need the guiding hand
To help us now and then
Here comes Sunday Silence again.

Every now and then it's hard to face,
There ain't no easy goin' in life's race
And when I'm feeling down and in defeat
The sound of Sunday Silence sure is sweet.

How my race will end Lord only knows
But when Sunday's here it's time to smell the rose
And stop and count the blessings that abound
In a place where Sunday Silence can be found.

Here comes Sunday Silence again
On the track of life sometimes you lose
Sometimes you win
We all need the guiding hand
To help us now and then
Here comes Sunday Silence
It's time for Sunday Silence
Here comes Sunday Silence again.

Someone who believes in omens like I do should not have been surprised. Before the Derby and the Preakness, there had been nothing but good omens. But between the Preakness and the Belmont things happened that I should not have overlooked.

About two weeks before the Belmont, I found a dead opossum on a farm road and got out to remove it. When I tugged it by the tail, three tiny babies came scrambling out from her pouch. I scooped them up and took them home to Staci who figured out how to feed them from a medicine dropper. But one morning when she checked on them, one had died. To me, the three had represented the Triple Crown. Bad omen.

We had three geese on the pond by our house and a few days before we went to New York, one of them disappeared. Again, bad omen.

Once we arrived in New York, with the prospect of winning the Triple Crown, I was invited on *Late Night with David Letterman* to talk about our chances. The other guests were Sammy Davis Jr. and the "Slug Lady," who had a vast collection of snails. I was scheduled to sing *Sunday Silence*, but the "Slug Lady" took up too much time showing Letterman her snails. I spent that time laughing and joking in the green room with Sammy Davis Jr. until I was called to go on the show to talk about the upcoming Belmont. I was nervous and he calmed me down. He told me I had two choices—my commitment or my fear.

The night before the big race, we were invited by Alex Campbell and David Reynolds to a dinner party for our entourage at Windows on the World in the North Tower of the World Trade Center. I have never seen such a view in all my life. There were floor to ceiling windows from which you could see all sides of New York City, as well as the Statue of Liberty and the other boroughs around Manhattan.

During cocktails, it began to rain, first as a drizzle and then in sheets. Everyone was celebrating the downpour. Sunday Silence

On Late Night with David Letterman – NBC

loved the off track—Easy Goer hated it. It seemed to be a sign that things could go our way for a win in the slop the next day.

While we were having dinner, I looked over my shoulder through the window and there were three huge moths huddling close together outside in a corner of the glass. I excitedly pointed them out to everyone and said, "This is a real omen—Triple Crown tomorrow!" But as we were having dessert, I looked out again and one of the moths had disappeared. I felt uneasy, and I remember Alex Campbell saying, "Hawk, you don't really believe those moths on the window have a damn thing to do with Sunday Silence winning the Triple Crown tomorrow, do you?"

We took the elevators all the way down to the first floor and when we went outside, low and behold, it was raining even harder. We were ecstatic. This foretold just what Sunday Silence wanted—a muddy track.

Charlie and Sunday Silence – Candice Rushing Photo

On the morning of the Belmont Stakes, everyone in the Sunday Silence camp was extremely optimistic. It had rained all night. Then about nine o'clock, Charlie called and was absolutely furious because the New York Racing Association had done something they *had never done in the history of the racetrack.* They closed the main track so they could dry it out for the big race. Every horse that morning had to train on the training track. Who ordered this and why is anybody's guess?

In the Derby and the Preakness, Easy Goer and Sunday Silence had run close races, with no more than a length or two separating them. But in the Belmont, on that dry home track, Easy Goer ran as never before. He roared past Sunday Silence in the stretch and won by eight lengths.

Aside from having just lost the Triple Crown, Sunday Silence also missed out on earning the five-million-dollar bonus that he would have received. In view of all the money I owed at the time, that would have been a godsend.

Other than the loss of a friend or family member, I was never so devastated. The impossible dream of winning the Triple Crown had slipped away. I suppose the higher the hopes, dreams and aspirations, the harder the fall when they are not realized.

Be that as it may, we had planned a "Win, Lose or Draw" dinner party at the 21 Club at eight o'clock that night. I have never dreaded going to anything more in my life than that dinner, but we had invited friends.

I had been counting on this being a happy celebration. Some guests were horse people who knew how bitter that loss was, like my longtime friend, Adger, and some industry leaders like Ted Bassett of Keeneland. They knew how badly I needed that bonus money.

There were some guests I thought might be just as uncomfortable as I was, maybe dreading it, too, since it was now a loser's party, like the Lexington sports radio personality Ralph Hacker and University of Kentucky basketball coach, Eddie Sutton.

The day after the Kentucky Derby, Hacker brought television personality Ralph Emery to the farm with Waylon Jennings and his wife, Jessi Colter. Staci and I showed them around, and then before the Preakness, Ralph invited me to be a guest on his show *Nashville Now*.

Before the Belmont, Ralph had invited me to be on his show again, and Waylon came to see me on the set. He suggested that he and I do a song together, *Good Hearted Woman*, the duet that had been a hit for him and Willie Nelson. He said I would do Willie's part.

It made me so nervous I wanted to crawl out of there.

Waylon noticed and said, "What's the matter with you, Hoss—you nervous?"

I said, "Man, I'm scared to death."

Then he said, "Hell, don't worry, Hoss. There's thirty million people watches this show, and everyone one of 'em's waitin' on you to fuck up." That actually calmed me down.

The song went great with just Waylon and I sitting there and him playing the guitar. When we finished, Ralph looked at Waylon and said, "What would Willie think?"

Waylon said, "It don't matter what Willie thinks—Willie don't have no horse!"

With Waylon Jennings singing Willie's part of Good Hearted Woman on *Nashville Now* before the Belmont Stakes in 1989 – The Country Music Hall of Fame

Now, they had all been invited to watch Sunday Silence hopefully win the Triple Crown, and they were among the guests at our dinner that night. Staci kept telling me to man up and be a good sport. After all, we had won the Derby and the Preakness.

But nothing could lift my spirits until Adger said, "At least you ran second and picked up the Triple Crown bonus of $500,000 for the most points in the series." Under the spell of my despair, I hadn't even thought of that.

When we arrived at the 21 Club, many of the guests were already there, all friendly faces, along with Jim McKay, host of ABC's *Wide World of Sports*, and his wife Margaret, Ralph and Marilyn Hacker, Eddie and Patsy Sutton, Staci's brother Brad and his wife Teri. Everybody but me was in a jubilant mood. I can still remember looking across the table and seeing Lucy Bassett having the best time talking to Waylon. Her husband, Ted, who was also head of the Breeders' Cup where we would next meet Easy Goer, was laughing and joking with Waylon's wife, Jessi. "The Ambassador" was entertaining people at the other end of the table with some good stories. It was soothing to be with friends.

Still, there seemed to be a dark cloud of depression hanging over me. And I had no idea that Ted Basset, anticipating the possible letdown inevitable at a victory party without a victory, had spotted a piano near the club entrance and convinced the management to have it delivered by elevator to our private dining room upstairs. He had already spoken to Jessi, and the next thing I knew she walked over to the piano and sat down. She looked across the room and said, "Arthur, this song is for you and Staci."

She told me to hold Staci's hand, and then sang one of her beautiful hit songs.

> *"Storms never last, do they, baby*
> *Bad times all pass with the wind*
> *Your hand in mine stills the thunder*
> *And you make the sun want to shine"*
> —JESSI COLTER

Like a fog lifting from a dark morning, my spirits began to rise and by the time she finished the song, I had tears in my eyes, and everything seemed okay. I felt a calm come over me and a sincere sense of gratitude for the incredible ride that Sunday Silence had given us. Hearing her song was one of the most uplifting moments ever for me.

Then she sang another of her hits, *I'm Not Lisa*. Our little dinner gathering went wild with applause. Waylon soon joined her, and they did some more classic songs together. The music of the night began healing the wounds of the day.

By that fall, we had lost two in a row, the Belmont and then the Swaps Stakes. The racing secretary at Santa Anita had talked Charlie into running Sunday Silence there against his better judgment. Then he went down for the Super Derby at Louisiana Downs, near where my great-grandfather, Captain Richard Hancock, was born and raised. He joined the Ninth Louisiana Regiment in Bogalusa at the start of the Civil War. His father, my great-great-grandfather Nathaniel Hancock, is buried six miles from the track in a field on the side of the road to nearby Minden, Louisiana. I thought that had to be a good omen.

We won the Super Derby by eight lengths and Sunday Silence was back to his devastating old self. That set him up for a final showdown with Easy Goer in the Breeders' Cup Classic at Gulfstream Park in Miami. Skeptics will scoff, but I like to think that my great-great-grandfather's karma helped to set Sunday Silence back on the right path.

My belief in superstition was probably a gift from Daddy. One time when we were at the races at Keeneland and were about to run a filly named Moccasin in a big stakes race, my father told me to sit in a certain seat and also told my mother and sister where they should sit. He was superstitious because we had been in those seats the last time she had run and won.

I said that I didn't think where we sat had anything to do with how she was going to run and I will never forget his reply: "You may be right, Bud—but I'm not going to tempt fate."

She won with ease.

Everything hinged on the next race—the Breeders' Cup Classic. The sportswriters were at it again. "If Easy Goer beats Sunday Silence in the Breeders' Cup, he'll win the three-year-old championship and be Horse of the Year." And he would have been, too.

I tried to come to grips with the possibility of getting beat by Mr. Phipps. He had helped my father and my family. He was a big part of Claiborne, and he was nice enough to have given me a job after college with his private trainer, Eddie Neloy. Our families had been entwined for decades, and I tried to tell myself that a win for Easy Goer would be a win for my family and Claiborne.

Ogden Mills "Dinny" Phipps was Ogden's only son. He and I had known each other most of our lives. He was a couple of years older and had been a very good tennis player at Yale when he was younger. He was in line to inherit the birthright of his family's dynasty, just as I had once been. But that was all we had in common.

One day, I was mucking out stalls in the Phipps's barn in New York. I was carrying a big burlap bag of manure on my back out to the muck pit. I was bent over from the weight, and it was raining and sleeting. As I sloshed through the mud, I thought to myself—this is a helluva thing to be doing with a BA in history from Vanderbilt.

About that time, a pink Cadillac drove by, and I looked sideways and saw a beautiful New York model glance at me as the car passed, hitting a puddle and splashing water on me and my muck sack. Since I was bent down, it got me head to toe. He didn't see me but driving the car was Dinny bringing this gorgeous girl out to see his horses.

That more or less set the tone for our relationship and to me was an apt metaphor for the trajectory of our lives.

About three weeks before the Breeders' Cup, seventeen years after my father died, Mr. Doug Parrish, who was one of Daddy's closest friends as well as an executor of my father's estate, pulled me aside at Louie's Restaurant and told me that he hoped that Sunday Silence would beat Ogden. He said it was Mr. Phipps who really wanted me to take a backseat to Seth at Claiborne. Mr. Doug said that Mr. Phipps was adamant that Claiborne needed a captain, and that Seth should be the one. I knew he told Seth that, but I had no idea the extent to which he apparently had fanned the flames against me. I don't know why Mr. Doug felt that he needed to tell me that after all that time, but he did.

The great sportswriter Bill Nack wrote a story in *Sports Illustrated* called "Blood Brothers in the Bluegrass" about Seth and me and the rivalry. When he interviewed me, I told him what I had just learned from Mr. Doug and he included it in his story.

These seventeen years later and three days before the Breeders' Cup on the backside of Gulfsteam, I was caught off guard to look up and see Dinny coming straight at me like a snorting bull. I knew right away something was up because he was breathing hard and glaring right through me. Being from Bourbon County, where violent physical confrontation is not all that rare, I knew we were about to get into it. I slipped my watch off my left wrist, put it in my pocket, and braced for the onslaught.

Dinny stopped about three feet in front of my face. He was so mad he was trembling. He said, "Who told you that it was my father who wanted you out of Claiborne?"

Ogden and Dinny Phipps - Barbara Livingston Photo

I looked him dead in the eye and answered, "It was my father's best friend, Doug Parrish, that's who."

His face became even more threatening, and he snarled, "Where does he bank?"

I said, "I've got no goddamned idea where he banks. What the hell is it to you?"

With that, he wheeled around and stormed away. By then, I was shaking as well, because my adrenaline was up. I started to say something but for once, I didn't.

Staci said, "Oh my God, Arthur, what was that all about?"

I was still in awe of Easy Goer. The first two races had been close. Then in the Belmont, he had run off and left us, which I could only blame on the fast track especially prepared for him. On the other hand, we had beaten him on dry tracks before, so maybe it was the extra quarter mile of the Belmont. Saturday arrived. The big day was at hand.

I felt better when Easy Goer was a step slow out of the gate. His rider, Pat Day liked to come from behind and blow past the leader at the end. That kind of ride had become his trademark that had jockeys in the lead looking back over their shoulders in the stretch expecting to see Day coming. Some called him Pat "Wait All Day."

Our jockey, Chris McCarron had zipped out of the eight hole and gotten himself a perfect spot up front, sitting third or fourth just off the leaders who were flying. Easy Goer was ten lengths behind going into the first turn, so I felt a glimmer of hope.

A speedball named Slew City Slew went the first quarter of a mile in twenty-two seconds and got the half in forty-six flat. A good horse named Blushing John was right on his hip, pushing him every stride.

They ran the first mile in a minute and thirty-five seconds, a killing pace. And our horse was just galloping easy right behind them.

Down the backstretch, Easy Goer was still in hand and hadn't even started to run. When the time came for them all to start for home, McCarron got the jump on Day and Easy Goer again. Sunday Silence was less bulky and sleeker on the turns and had kept his lead on Easy Goer while the leaders were tiring from the frantic battle up front. When Slew City Slew finally ran out of steam and Blushing John took the lead, Sunday Silence was in full speed closing like he did in the Derby and the Preakness. I thought we had it.

On my knees praying that Easy Goer won't catch Sunday Silence at the wire of the 1989 Breeders' Cup Classic. Next to me is Staci and friend Norma Thurman. Second Row from left, John Fischer, Alex Campbell, John Adger and our banker, Willie Rouse – NBC Sports

Dark Horses – The Tony Leonard Collection

With Eclipse Awards won by Sunday Silence – Champion Three Year Old Colt and 1989 Horse of the Year
– Bert Morgan Photo

Then I heard the great race caller Tom Durkin say, "Sunday Silence is bracing for the oncoming power of Easy Goer." All of a sudden there he was, and my heart was in my throat. That great racehorse was rolling like a runaway train, gaining ground with every jump. I dropped down on my knees in the front of the box, praying, "Please God, don't let this big red sonofabitch catch us," and for a minute I thought he might. But he didn't get there in time.

That was it. The championship was decided. Sunday Silence prevailed by a neck. We'd won the Derby and Preakness and had now beaten Easy Goer in the final showdown. We would be three-year-old champion and Horse of the Year. We were headed to the winners' circle while Mr. Phipps was heading to his car. Nothing was ever said between us again. The slate was wiped clean.

THE BOY THAT HE FIRED

Seventeen years ago to this day
The great Ogden Phipps had his own way,
And banished young Arthur off on his own
To face the cold world, crushed and alone.

The man called him wild and not the right lad
To run Claiborne Farm and follow his dad.
For he was quite clever and smart and he knew
That Arthur would run it like he wanted to.

Seventeen years thus came and then passed
Till fate sent to Phipps the big horse at last.
He had his best steed since the Buckpasser day
And seemed to have everything going his way.

He thought that success and great victory were his
But sadly for him, it has now come to this.
For money and power and all he'd acquired
Could not put a stop to the boy that he fired.

What goes around comes around, remember it well
The angels in heaven have their tale to tell
And ere you would harm an innocent soul
Take heed, there are some things beyond your control.

The dream that you take from a heart full of joy
May someday haunt you or your own little boy,
And steal from your life something you most desired
Through righteous revenge for the boy that you fired.

For nothing can hinder the pathway of fate
As destiny dawns, be it early or late.
Phipps should have known how the young lad was sired
And kept him around, the boy that he fired.

CHAPTER 18

The Sale of Sunday Silence

FOLLOWING THE BREEDERS' CUP, we gave Sunday Silence a rest until June third, 1990 when he won his first start as a four year old in the Californian.

After the race, we were approached by the Yoshida family of Shadai Farm to whom we sold a quarter interest for 2.5 million dollars. The Hancock family had a long history with the Yoshida family. In the early 70s, my father sold them Hutchison Farm in Paris which my grandfather had left to my Aunt Nancy, Daddy's sister. Zenya Yoshida's son, Teruya, had come to Paris to run it, and we became friends. Teruya is a good guitar player and singer in his own right, as well as a consummate horseman.

On June 24th, Sunday Silence came back in the Hollywood Gold Cup. I was there in the paddock when Charlie very distinctly told Patrick Valenzuela five times not to use the whip. Five times! Charlie pointed one by one to each of his five fingers saying clearly "Patrick, do not use the whip." . . . Sunday Silence was beaten by a head when Patrick went to his whip down the stretch.

A match race with Easy Goer, The Arlington Challenge, was planned for later in the summer but never materialized because both horses sustained career-ending injuries leading up to the race. The decision was made to bring Sunday Silence back to Stone Farm to become a stallion.

Nobody had wanted Sunday Silence as a young horse, and now nobody wanted to breed to him either. Given that I owed $15 million, I had no choice but to sell him. The bankers were breathing down my neck.

Even champion racehorses have only about a fifty percent chance of making it as a top sire. Daddy said one out of two make it, and he needs to be a horse with a lot of ability, good conformation, and a hell of a pedigree. Sunday Silence had a lot of ability, but not the best conformation, and not a lot of pedigree.

In 1990, almost none of the American breeders would take shares in Sunday Silence. I called everybody I knew in the horse world and found only three people who would take one. Nobody wanted him. It broke my heart.

One day I got a call from Suzanne McNew representing the Yoshidas. She said they would like to buy the entire horse. I was shocked and asked her what price they had in mind?

She said $10 million cash and that I would be compensated $750,000 for the value of my four breeding rights to stand Sunday Silence at Stone Farm, and that Charlie would be compensated $187,500 for his for having trained the horse.

God knows, I didn't want to sell Sunday Silence, but I asked some very smart businessmen and they all said selling was the wise thing to do. When I saw my father's friend and my mentor, Warner Jones, at the Keeneland September Yearling Sale, I told him of the $10 million offer, my inability to syndicate him, and asked him what he thought.

At Santa Anita with Zenya Yoshida and his son Teruya in 1990 – Shigeki Kikkawa Photo

Mr. Jones, who owned Hermitage Farm and was chairman of Churchill Downs, was also a very wise horseman and businessman. He jumped up from his chair and said, "Where are they right now?" I told Mr. Jones that my friend Teruya and his father Zenya were somewhere on the sales grounds.

He said, in no uncertain terms, "Find them and make that deal right now! It's better to sell and be sorry than to keep and be sorry."

My dear friend Bill Young, one of the leading businessmen in America, also advised me to sell. He said "When you're in debt, you're a slave. You can take that money, pay down the bank, and upgrade your broodmare band." And as my father would have said, "bigger boats may venture more, but smaller boats should stay near shore."

The day we put Sunday Silence on the van to send him to Japan, I cried for the first time in years. He had saved our farm and family.

Now we had to let him go because none of the American breeders wanted him. There was no way on earth we could afford to keep him. The dark horse found a home at last. But I will always deeply regret that it could not have been at Stone Farm. Between racing earnings and his sale, the overall benefit of Sunday Silence to his owners was north of $15 million. Time would show that even at the price they paid, the Yoshidas made one of the greatest bargains ever in the history of the breed.

Sunday Silence and our family at Stone Farm – The Tony Leonard Collection

LAWYERS

In the course of peaceful life
There comes the time of sickly strife
When misery is on the throne
And trouble won't leave us alone
Oppression, tax, and daily blues
Cost us precious lifeblood dues
When from his high-rise lofty perch
From his shadowed leather lurch
Comes the parasite on his journey
The maggot of man, nicknamed "attorney"
And while his fellow man is down
And darkness and despair abound
The maggot begins to interview
Alternatives, pay or sue
Then to the feeding ground—the court
Where the maggot laughs and jests in sport
Viewed by the tick, omnipotent judge
It's like a fat man eating fudge
This hoax that wanes so terribly vile
Thus gains respect and is called a trial
The tick leans back and frowns his face
Then sums it up the victim's case
And like a chicken who's just been picked
The client in silence is told the verdict
The poor man leaves, was justice done?
His money spent, his race is run
Bitter tears and unhealed scars . . .
While the maggot lounges in local bars
Spending the money he has made
Because his neighbor was afraid
Live off misfortune, death, and shame
Play if you like, the lawyer's game

A few months after we sold Sunday Silence, I was in California at a horse sale and a big, rough-looking guy who looked like a hit man came up to me and asked me if I was Arthur Hancock. I said I was, and he reached into his coat. Instead of pulling a weapon, he handed me a summons. I was being sued by Dr. Ernest Gaillard, to whom Charlie had sold twenty-five of his fifty percent interest in the horse. Our partner thought he was entitled to a part of the compensation I had received for my breeding rights, although he did not sue Charlie for his.

The racing partnership agreement Paul had drawn up stipulated that if there was ever a dispute or a lawsuit, the loser would have to pay the attorney fees of the winner. Paul found me a lawyer in California named Bob Forgnone, who was brilliant. It took four years, but the judge threw the case out on a summary judgment. I had spent $187,500 defending myself and Forgnone told Dr. Gaillard he needed to bring in a check.

Dr. Gaillard came into Forgnone's office one day and threw a $25,000 check on his desk and said, "That's all I'm paying."

Forgnone called me and asked if I would like to handle the situation in a gentlemanly manner or take whatever legal remedies were available—although it might not be pleasant. I urged him to do everything as ungentlemanly and unpleasantly as possible.

Forgnone took several courses of action, the first of which was to put some social pressure on Dr. Gaillard through another attorney who knew him. But Gaillard wouldn't budge. Then he discovered that Forgone was pulling out all of the stops. So he came in with another check for $15,000 and said, "That's the last payment you're ever going to get, and if you don't take it I will fight you to the end over it."

Forgnone told him, "With all due respect, Dr. Gaillard, what are you going to fight with? As of noon today, you won't have a house, an office building, a car, or a bank account. I've had the US Marshals attach everything you own until you pay Mr. Hancock what you owe him under the terms of the contract."

Gaillard almost exploded, but shortly thereafter forked over the balance he owed—and that was that.

For a $25,000 investment, he had made over three and a half million and still wanted more. When Sunday Silence sold, I got $750,000 for my breeding rights and $5 million for my half. That was a huge cash infusion. And he also had won close to $5 million. I had a half of that minus trainer and jockey commissions, which amounted to roughly another $2 million. So, about $8 million dollars came to us from Sunday Silence. As I have said, he saved me, our family, and our farm. God had answered my prayer.

Case closed—I was saved from bankruptcy. But there's another dear friend to whom I'm grateful for helping to complete my redemption.

Paul Sullivan had written me a long letter in his own hand that also helped save my business and allow me to live long enough to see my grandchildren and write this book.

His advice was to simply to return to the business practices that had made my father and grandfather so successful. Sell the land I did not need, all the horses that had not been profitable, and resume partnerships with lucky and successful people. He said to quit playing around in the 'Sport of Kings' and go back to good, sound business principles.

His letter changed the way I had been doing things and set me on a path to survival in the extraordinarily challenging endeavor of raising Thoroughbreds. It was a blessing then and a treasure today. Wisdom is the greatest gift one friend can bestow or receive from another.

So, before relinquishing his interest in Sunday Silence, Paul had asked three wise friends their opinions. A top Irish bloodstock agent named Billy McDonald told him the horse was "a triple zero." Elaine "Legs" Lawlor, a respected Irish horsewoman, totally concurred with Billy. Mary Bradley, a well-known California owner told Paul she wouldn't pay the training bills on the horse even if he gave him to her.

To have some fun with Paul, who had never even once whimpered about having sold his interest, I wrote the following poem from my perspective as "the coon," with Paul as "the fox," Billy as "the warthog," Legs as "the crane," and Mary as "the bear."

With my old pal Paul – Hancock Family Photo

FOXED AGAIN

A fox and a coon sat under the moon,
Each eyeing a fresh piece of meat.
The fox wasn't sure that the morsel was pure,
While the coon was convinced it was sweet.

So the fox asked the warthog, the crane, and the bear,
To give him their thoughts on the meal.
While the coon sniffed the scent of a feast in the air,
They told him to turn down the deal.

Now the meat was quite high on a mountain nearby,
And 'twould have to be carried afar.
And the fox was convinced that the work it commenced,
Was not worth the time or the mar.

He said to the coon, whom he thought a buffoon,
"You eat, and all will be well.
If I share the meal, it will spoil the whole deal,
And the feast will turn out to be hell."

But the coon begged his friend to help and stay in,
Yet all this was to no avail.
And the more he beseeched, the more the fox screeched,
And leapt in the air and turned tail.

Now under the moon sits the fat cunning coon,
And he really does think it's a shame,
That his buddy, old red, heeded what others said,
And the fox was outfoxed, at his own foxing game!

CHAPTER 19

"Fu Peg"

OFTEN DURING THE LAST fifty years, people have heard me say, "Thank God and John Adger," without having a clue as to what I was talking about.

Since our first duck-hunting trip when we were in our twenties, John has been a steadfast supporter of Stone Farm and has assisted and advised me in "horse trading" in too many ways to mention. He brokered the purchase of Goodbye Halo who went on to win the Kentucky Oaks for the farm and Alex Campbell. He helped me acquire Northern Baby to stand at the farm. It seemed that John knew everyone in the horse business and was always quick with an introduction to Stone Farm.

One of the most important good turns came in 1994 when John asked me to come down to Houston and meet Bob and Janice McNair, who were interested in getting into the horse business. John was going to advise them.

He threw a little dinner party for us, and we all had a fabulous time together. They asked me some questions about the horse industry, and I told them my opinions and philosophies. Bob said they were interested in getting only a few horses and perhaps some in partnership with me, which was indeed a very nice compliment. Bob was interested in the sporting aspect of racing and Janice was a genuine horse lover. It wasn't long until we began our association and from day one it was a successful relationship.

The first partnership was in a horse we owned with Charlie named Strodes Creek. He had just finished third in the 1991 Santa Anita Derby, and we had already been offered $1.8 million for him, so on John's advice the McNairs bought a third interest for $600,000. Only weeks later, he ran second in the Kentucky Derby—a pretty good start for our new racing endeavor!

That was the beginning. The McNairs and I were extremely lucky together and had a world of success, in large part due to the advice of Adger, "The Ambassador".

One of the mares we decided to purchase in partnership was a recently retired racing filly named Angel Fever from the dispersal of John Ed Anthony's Loblolly Stable. She was very good-looking, a full sister to John Ed's Preakness winner Pine Bluff, and a half-sister to his Arkansas Derby winner Demons Begone. Dr. Gary Lavin, who advised John Ed, told us that not only was Angel Fever the best racing filly they had ever owned, she was the best racehorse, period. We had great respect for John Ed and his accomplishments as a breeder, so we decided to bid on her.

I did the bidding and what I intended to be my final bid was $475,000. Then someone topped me at $500,000 which scared me off. That was out of my league and when asked for another bid, I shook my head no. John repeated to Bob who was sitting beside me what Gary Lavin had said about her being John Ed's best racehorse, and Bob said to me, "Arthur, if she's worth $500,000 surely she's worth $25,000 more."

That sounded logical so I bid $525,000 and we got her! If not for the encouragement from Bob and John, I would have stopped.

We bred her to Mr. Prospector who was a wonderful stallion standing at Claiborne. The first foal we got was a filly that we sold for a million dollars, which was a record price for a weanling filly at the time.

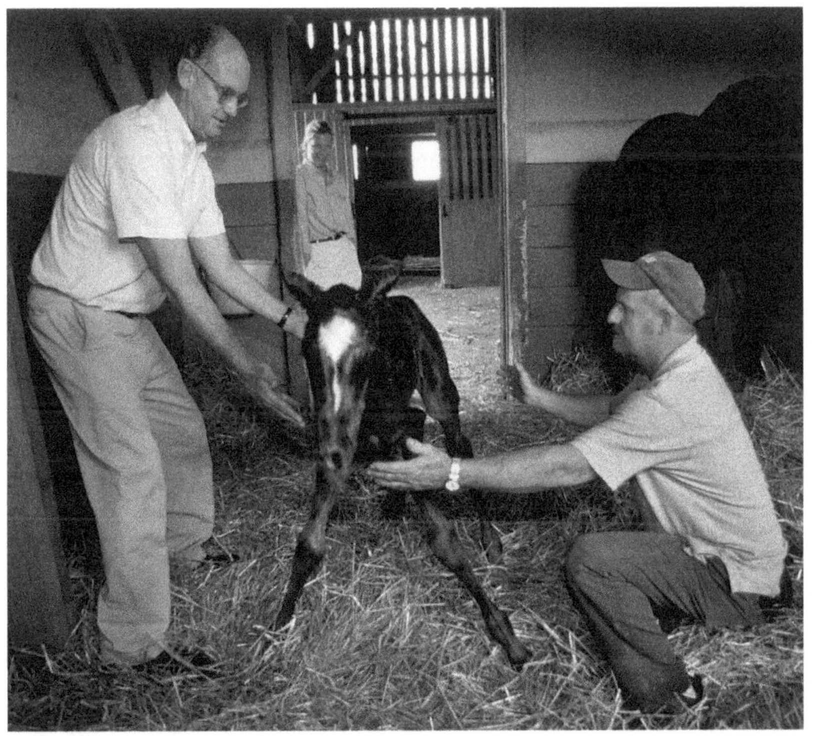

Staci watching Everett Charles and me trying to steady a newborn foal – Mellisa Farlow Photo

I was at the foaling barn when Angel Fever's next offspring was born. I had never seen such a colt in all my life. I would still say he was the best-looking foal I have ever seen, so good-looking that I gave him the nickname "Superman".

Not only was he a gorgeous, well-muscled, and perfectly proportioned foal, he was highly intelligent as well. The night he was born he raised up and looked at all five of us who were standing around him, just like a dog would look at you, from one person to the next. He seemed amazed that he was in this new world. I even commented to everybody how unusual it was that a newborn foal would scrutinize each of us individually, sizing us up one at a time.

As Superman grew up, he showed his intelligence time and time again. One particular day when he was a young foal, he was out in the paddock with his mother. A storm blew up and he began rearing and pawing at the lightning and thunder as the rain descended upon him. Another time when he was a yearling, the snow was waist deep in the barn lot. As I led him out to wade through it, he stopped and stood still, carefully studying it before he would move forward.

He was also very curious and would leave the other horses in the field to come and check you out if you entered his domain. He was clearly the alpha of the pack.

About a week before he was to be sold, I was in my office on the phone with Chris Williams from Nashville. I told Chris we had a marvel of nature going to the sale. No sooner than the words left my mouth than a huge bolt of lightning hit a tree close to my window knocking off a massive limb. The crack was so loud and the light so bright that I leapt to my feet. Chris heard it over the phone and said, "What in the hell was that, Hawk?" I told him and he said with a laugh, "Maybe you'd better not sell him."

When we took him to the Keeneland July Yearling Sale, word quickly spread that he was the best-looking colt in the sale. There was a lot of buzz about him and when he came into the ring, he had the look of a general overseeing the battlefield, or what we call in the horse business, "the look of eagles."

His beautiful bay coat shined and glistened like polished bronze, thanks to the great work of our farm manager John Hayes and his groom, Everett "Powell County" Charles.

I was confident we had at least two very powerful, separate bidders. Then, Adger came in and sat down beside me and said, "Oh no! Oooh no!"

I said, "What the hell's the matter with you?" He told me to look across the sales pavilion. What I saw were our two "money men" who had teamed up and were obviously going to bid on the horse as partners. They were Satish Sanan, an Indian-born technology entrepreneur, and the Irish powerhouse Coolmore. They would now most likely be bidding against the Arabs. They never missed spotting a good horse. But this would likely limit the number of bidders at the top end and could cost us dearly. I had thought we were going to get a good price, hopefully $2 million, but after seeing them sitting together, I wasn't so sure.

What we didn't know at the time was that another prominent horseman from Bourbon County, trainer John T. Ward, had orders from his Japanese client Fusao Sekiguchi to "buy the best horse in the sale." John had already set his sights on our Angel Fever colt.

The bidding began and escalated past our $2 million goal, even before Ward made his first bid against our "money men." It turned out that his instructions were, "Go to two million and then ask."

The "money men" kept bidding. Ward and Sekiguchi kept nodding, and the hushed crowd watched in awe as the hammer fell after a final bid of $4 million. We were ecstatic as the press gathered around to ask us how we felt. It was an electric evening that also meant further security for the farm.

After the sale, when I went to thank Mr. Sekiguchi, he told me, "I not be conquered . . . I prevail."

His instincts proved to be correct. The colt became a very good racehorse and was pointed to the Kentucky Derby with his big prep race being the Wood Memorial at Belmont Park in New York. He won the Wood very easily and was one of the favorites for the Derby under the careful conditioning of Hall-of-Fame trainer Neil Drysdale, who ironically had been the top assistant to Charlie Whittingham for years.

A couple of days after the Wood, back at the farm, there were about seven of us at the barn right by the stall where he was foaled and I said, "Wouldn't it be something if Superman won the Kentucky Derby." As if on cue, a big, beautiful red fox came flying around the barn at full speed, running right through the barn lot past us, and diving sideways through another fence. Then he went full speed out across the big field disappearing into the woods. I said, "Boys, if that's not an omen I've never seen one. He will win the Kentucky Derby."

And that is exactly what Fusaichi Pegasus did. After his great racing career and because of his good looks, racing ability, and his pedigree, Coolmore finally did purchase him, this time for north of $70 million.

Sometime later, Mr. Sekiguchi came for a visit to Stone Farm. While there, he congratulated me on breeding and raising his champion, who by this time was famous in the industry as "Fu Peg."

He said, "Arthur-san, you are a genius."

I said, "Mr. Sekiguchi, you bought a horse from us for 4 million dollars, won the Kentucky Derby with him, and then sold him for over $70 million. You, Mr. Sekiguchi, are the genius!"

In the tradition of his country, Mr. Sekiguchi thanked me for the compliment by bowing several times and repeating, "Ah . . . ha ha . . . Athuh-san— Ah . . . ha ha, Athuh-san." Then we all laughed like hell.

The McNairs and Staci and I had a wonderful partnership, and we were extremely blessed and lucky together. We have John Adger to thank for it all.

"Superman" Fusaichi Pegasus winning the 2000 Kentucky Derby — Bill Straus Photo

The McNairs ended up owning about two dozen horses, which we boarded for them at Stone Farm, as well as the mares we had in partnership together. Bob had also said that the last thing he ever wanted was a farm. But as the horse numbers increased, it occurred to them that getting their own place might be a good idea.

Remembering Paul's good advice in his letter that the 4,600 acres I owned at the time was much more land than I needed, I sold the McNairs Stonerside Farm, 1,248 acres of classic horse country land that had about a mile of frontage on Highway 460, while beautiful Stoner Creek ran down the entire backside of the farm.

This was the farm that had made Stone Farm bigger than Claiborne. I bought it after Gato Del Sol won the Derby in 1982. I had really bitten off more than I could chew, and it was one of the reasons why I amassed so much debt over the next few years.

We had put a fair price on Stonerside and Bob and Janice made it into an absolute showplace. My father had a saying that "for a deal to be a good deal, it has to be good for both parties" and that's what the sale of Stonerside meant for both of us. They acquired a beautiful farm, and the sale enabled me to eliminate a lot of debt, worry, and expense.

Bob and Janice fixed up the beautiful old home and raised so many good horses on this farm that it eventually attracted the attention of Sheikh Mohammed, the ruler of Dubai. Around the same time, Bob acquired the Houston pro football franchise and named the team the Houston Texans. So, when Sheikh Mohammed made him an offer he couldn't refuse, Bob decided to concentrate on football, and sell the farm and the horses in a package deal orchestrated by Adger and Sullivan.

Looking back, we all had a lot of fun together. One time, Bob flew into Lexington in his Challenger with Adger on board to pick me up along with Paul and my son Arthur to fly north to see the Houston Texans play the Indianapolis Colts. When we landed, we had a police escort taking us from the airport to the stadium. Somewhere en route, Paul quipped, "Bob, the sirens are making Arthur nervous." Bob said, "Why is Arthur nervous, Paul?" and Paul replied, "because the sirens are usually behind him."

CHAPTER 20

Reminiscing

I THINK OF MAMA every day. I remember the nights she'd stay up and comfort me when, as a child, my asthma would flare up and I could hardly breathe, or the times I was ill, and she'd stay at my bedside and nurse me back to health. I also remember her strict discipline when I was bad and she'd say, "Ahhthuh, go get me a switch." The worst time was when I lied to her after she told me not to eat any of the sugar cookies in a big glass jar. She asked me if I had gotten one and I said "no ma'am." Little did I know that she had counted them. She told me to go get her a switch. "Don't you evuh, evuh lie to me again", she said as she thrashed my bare legs. And I didn't.

Mama had wonderful common sense, and she always gave me good advice whenever I'd ask her about something. She would have made an A-plus in logic. Mama was one of a kind, a great character with a keen sense of humor.

My mother was my father's partner in rebuilding Claiborne back into the legendary farm it had been before my grandfather had become ill. Nobody was more charming or a better hostess. In the early days, when hotel rooms were scarce in central Kentucky, the farm's clients would stay at Claiborne House for two or three days when they would come to see their horses. My father would impart his knowledge and show them their horses during the day, while Mama would treat them to lunch and seated dinners laced with wine and lively conversation.

Mama – Keeneland Library Collection

The day my mother died was the saddest day of my life. After the funeral and a gathering of some close friends and relatives at Claiborne House, I came back to Stone Farm and went in the library. I opened the case of my Martin D-35 guitar, and sitting there by myself sang, *Will the Circle Be Unbroken.* I played the whole song with tears streaming down my face.

Then I put on my bathing suit and went down to the pool. It was a beautiful day, and I needed to be alone. I decided to check the skimmer boxes for leaves before lying down on the warm slate to try and relax in the sun. I was hoping to get some relief from the overwhelming sadness and the realization that Mama was gone forever.

I opened the first of two skimmer boxes, and something happened that scared the hell out of me and caused me to jump back three feet. As I bent over, straight up out of the water and right toward my face came a head about the size of my fist. I was sure that a big snake was striking at me. Just as I jumped away, it landed on the ground, and I was shocked at what I saw.

It was the biggest bullfrog I'd ever seen in my life, and I had seen literally hundreds of them. We used to gig frogs when I was a child, and I can still remember opening the refrigerator door one morning to check on the dead frogs that my father had put there in a sack. One jumped right out at my face that day, too.

But this one was twice the size of any frog I had ever seen. And it had beautiful golden green skin that dazzled in the sun. Then it jumped about six feet back into the middle of the pool, swam underwater down to the deep end, and stopped on the bottom.

I felt comforted knowing that Mama had always had an affinity for paintings and statues of frogs. I was so emotionally and physically worn out that I lay down to relax in the warm summer sun before going in the water to get the bullfrog and put him back in the lake below the house. I had done this many times before and I always enjoyed swimming underwater trying to beat the frogs at their own game. The bigger ones were always the fastest, and I figured this frog would be a major challenge.

It must've been ninety degrees, and after only about five minutes, I was so uncomfortable that I decided to dive in and catch the frog. I stood up and looked in the pool and there was nothing there. I thought maybe I was at a bad angle and walked down to the deep end and checked both skimmer boxes—still no frog. He had disappeared.

There is no way that frog could've gotten out of that pool because there is a concrete lip over the edges. I was spooked and walked all the way around the pool again looking for a possible water trail or some other clue as to how the frog had vanished. I even wondered if a hawk could have swooped down and grabbed him, but I would have heard the commotion.

I have thought about that frog many times over the years and to this day, I have no idea how that golden, gleaming, gigantic frog vanished from the pool. It may sound crazy, but I believe it was Mama's spirit reminding me that she was still with me.

THE SNOWS OF DECEMBER

When the snows come down in December
And the wind makes the lonesomest sound
I long for my mama and I miss her
But Mama's in the cold, cold ground.

There's no one to help me and guide me
The rock that I leaned on is gone
I always could turn to my mama
But now her sweet spirit has flown.

The light of my life was Mama
And Lord how I miss her today
When the snows come down in December
For comfort and solace I pray.

But there is one promise that is given
Written in the scripture so plain
The promise made by our redeemer
Someday I'll see Mama again.

The light of my life was Mama
And Lord how I miss her today
When the snows come down in December
For comfort and solace I pray.
For comfort and solace I pray.

Charlie Whittingham was a redemptive force in my life and a father figure when I really needed one. I've always thought that one could live life by old sayings and Charlie certainly had his share, which he would often repeat to me:

"Never say anything bad about a horse until he's been dead at least ten years."

"If foresight was hindsight, we'd be better off by a damned sight."

"I taught him everything he knows—but not everything I know."

"I showed him where Molly put the peaches."

"Hope for the best and be prepared for the worst."

"Nobody knows but Whitey and Mose—and they're both dead."

"He who hoots with owls, cannot soar with eagles."

My friend James E. "Ted" Bassett, legendary chairman of Keeneland and a true world ambassador for Thoroughbred Racing, is an expert on many subjects, none more than aging. In October of 2024, he celebrated his 103nd birthday. Ted always says that "Age is a matter of the mind, and if you don't mind, it doesn't matter."

Looking back over my eight decades on this earth, it is impossible to remember every mile of this wonderful journey called life. Some of us learn the easy way and some the hard way, but the main thing is that we learn. I have made many mistakes, but I can say I have learned from them all. That's one of the keys to life, I think.

LOOK AT ME SEE ME

Look at me see me growing old
Leaving all behind
Sweet happy days now long gone by
Passing through my mind
Little childish hopes and dreams
Have vanished one by one
Friends and ladies so fond of me
Their happy smiles have flown

Look at me see me growing old
There's nothing that can be done
I must go where I was before
Far beyond the sun
To a place we know not of
Nor yet can even dream
To join the ones who have gone before
And one we've never seen

Look at me see me growing old
The time will soon come round
When all that will be left of me
No longer can be found
But finding strength in the joys behind
And hope in the world ahead
Will rest my body and soothe my mind
Till from this planet I've fled
Look at me see me growing old
Leaving all behind, leaving all behind

One Christmas, when I was at prep school, the rest of the boys had gone home except me and three others who had accumulated a number of demerits. We had to stay a couple of extra days and work them off. So, Mr. Latham, who taught English, took us way up a winding dirt road into the Blue Ridge Mountains with bread and canned goods to give to the mountain people who were very needy.

I remember going into a little cabin where there was a man, his wife, and five children. It was a scene that instantly reminded me of the random good fortune of my own life. These people had nothing.

One of the girls was about my age. I looked over on one of the beds in a dark corner and saw movement. There was a 500-pound hog lying on it. I asked the girl what they were going to do with the hog. She flashed a pretty smile and said, "We gonna eateem."

We wished them a Merry Christmas and left, but to this day I have never forgotten the girl and the hog. I got on the old George Washington train that night and arrived the next morning back home at Claiborne and the lovely old house where I was raised. There is a Kristofferson song that reminds me of how I felt that day—*Why Me, Lord?* What stroke of destiny and fate put me where I was and that beautiful girl in that cabin with a hog?

Bob Kleberg, who owned the world-famous King Ranch, would come to visit my father from time to time. Daddy said he was a real cowboy. And he was. I once set four soup cans on a fence, and he unerringly shot them off with a pistol.

I had watched Roy Rogers and other westerns and I always felt that if somebody tried to lasso me, I would just knock the rope away when it went over my head. So, I told Mr. Kleberg that. He said, "Well, by God, after lunch we'll just go outside and see what you can do." I was gonna show him.

He lined up about twenty yards away and told me to run from one tree to the other. He had the lasso twirling around in the air, and I took off running at full speed. The next thing I knew he had thrown the rope right in front of where I was about to land and when I did, he roped both legs and jerked me off my feet. Then he came over laughing and tied me up like he would a steer. My father walked up and looked down at me on the ground and said, "You see, Arthur, you're not so damned smart as you think you are."

I always had to try to prove or disprove every theory I was ever taught about breeding and raising horses. And sometimes it worked out in my favor.

That's what I tried to do early on in the horse business, breed good horses from cheap horses. I should have written a song called *The Underdog*, because I always identified as one. As Kristofferson wrote in his song *The Pilgrim*, "*He's a walking contradiction, partly truth and partly fiction, taking every wrong direction on his lonely way back home.*" Maybe that's why I identified with Sunday Silence. We were both underdogs, dark horses.

Even in the face of all my mistakes, I have somehow emerged physically intact and financially sound. I have no idea why I was allowed to come out virtually unscathed from all the scrapes I seemed to have had a knack for getting myself into.

When I left Claiborne Farm and my heritage, I was content, if necessary, to farm the hundred leased acres that I had at the time. I figured if I failed in the horse business, I would live a quiet life, working on the farm, reading some good books, playing some good music, and not having too much stress. But little did I know, it wasn't meant to be.

Four years after leaving and going on my own, in October of 1976, I was invited by Alec and Ghislaine Head to go to the biggest race in Europe to watch a filly my father had bred run in the prestigious Arc de Triomphe. The filly named Ivanjica won the race, and the celebration was unbelievable. It was a who's who of celebrities from Europe. Alec Head trained her, and his son Freddie rode her. The caviar and French champagne were flowing. It was a big change for me after working seven days a week on my little farm and it gave me a glimpse of what being successful was like. Not only was Alec Head one of the world's greatest horsemen, he was one of the most attractive and charming men I've had the good fortune to know. His *joie de vivre* was second to none.

When I got back home, I wrote a song about the trip and the filly called *Goodbye Ivanjica.* I finished it up one night about ten o'clock, along with a bottle of wine. I phoned Alec and sang it for him. It didn't dawn on me that it was three a.m. in Chantilly, France. He said, "Sounds good, Arthur . . . now I'm going back to sleep." I finished another verse and another glass and woke him up a second time twenty minutes later. Alec always got a kick out of that and over the years, we had many a good laugh about it.

Wayne Shumate was a dear friend of mine from right here in Paris, Kentucky. I told him a story that he loved, which was an allegory about picking up that first drink.

A man was walking down a cold dark road when he came upon a poisonous snake. The snake said, "Please pick me up and warm me. I am dying out here in the cold." The man said, "If I pick you up and warm you, you will bite me, and I will die." The snake said, "Oh no, I would never do that if you saved my life." Feeling sorry for him, the man picked up the snake and put him in his jacket. Somewhere down the road, he felt a searing pain in his side and threw the snake on the ground. Then he said to him, "How could you do this to me? I warmed you and saved your life and now you have bitten me and I'll never see my family again." The snake sneered up at him and hissed, "You knew what I was when you picked me up."

Right before Christmas in 2003, after I had been sober for fifteen years, I told Wayne I was planning to have a glass of eggnog on Christmas Day just like Daddy had made it—with a fifth of bourbon whiskey and a fifth of rum mixed into our homemade eggnog. I was adamant that I was going to pour myself a julep cup and stand by the crackling fireplace, just as Dad and I had done on many a Christmas past. I said, "There's no turning back, Wayne, so don't try to talk me out of it."

He said, "Well just remember one thing."

I looked at him and sarcastically replied, "And just what is that, Mr. Sage of Wisdom."

Wayne replied, "Remember, Hawk, that snake is coiled up down in that eggnog."

That chilled me to the bone, and I haven't thought about taking a drink since.

I GAVE IT ALL UP FOR THE BOTTLE

I could have been the hero of my high school football team
I might have wed the sweetest girl the world has ever seen
I could have done a thousand things and be held in esteem
But I gave it all up for the bottle

They said I had potential, I could have it all someday
But life was just a game to me that I was born to play
And all in all and through it all, I threw it all away
I gave it all up for the bottle

I gave it all up for the bottle
The one true friend I thought I had
Who would not let me down
Running in the fast lane
With my foot down on the throttle
I gave it all up for the bottle

Now here I stand a broken man, I hope it's not too late
To make amends, start again, and try to set things straight
I've been a prisoner far too long, dying to escape
From the demon who lives inside the bottle

I gave it all up for the bottle
The one true friend I thought I had
Who would not let me down
Running in the fast lane
With my foot down on the throttle
I gave it all up for the bottle
I gave it all up . . . for the bottle

Prince Fahd bin Salman of Saudi Arabia was an avid horseman and the son-in-law of Khalid bin Abdullah, the owner of Juddmonte Farms in Lexington. We met Prince Fahd in 1993 during the Saratoga Yearling Sale through his English trainer, Paul Cole, and his bloodstock advisor, Anthony Penfold. We all joined his dinner party one night after the sales at historic Siro's, which was known for its late-night dinners that ran well into the morning hours. The following year, he invited us to dinner at Juddmonte and asked us to fly with him on his massive 747 from Lexington to Washington, D.C. the next day. Seven black limousines met us and Fahd's other guests and took us to the Four Seasons Hotel where the prince had reserved the entire top floor. He took me to a room that was in direct contact with Riyadh, Saudi Arabia.

Later that night, he took us all out to dinner at a lovely restaurant in Alexandria. He asked me to play *Sunday Silence* for his daughter and sent his valet, Robert, out on the street where he gave a man $500 for what appeared to be a thirty-dollar guitar. The owner of the guitar was ecstatic. Robert brought it back in the restaurant, and I took it and sang the song to her with about twenty other guests listening at our table. By the time I sang the last verse, she had tears streaming down her face.

That spring, Strodes Creek was running in the Triple Crown series. Fahd became interested in buying a piece of him, and he asked us to be his guests at his stately home in England for the 1994 Royal Ascot race meet. A year before, I had sold some paintings by John Herring Sr. at Sotheby's to pay a bank note. One of them was of a gray horse with a gray cat in a manger, which I always associated with Gato Del Sol and the gray cat in the sun. Staci and I could hardly believe it when we saw it in Prince Fahd's home.

The day we were leaving, Fahd led us to the hallway where it was hanging and ceremoniously took it off the wall and handed it to me saying, "This came from your house to my house, and you bought it because of your Kentucky Derby winner. It belongs in your house."

I said, "Thank you so very much, Fahd. I will send you a check."

He said, "Absolutely not. This is destiny, from your house to my house, from my house to your house. Things go full circle."

I said, "Prince Fahd, maybe coincidence and destiny are brothers."

One afternoon at Royal Ascot, Staci and I were invited to have tea with the Queen and the Queen Mother. It was indeed an honor to see the Queen again and to be included in such an illustrious group. I was seated right next to the Queen Mother, who was 94 at the time. She was a most fascinating lady with a wonderful sense of humor, and we shared some delightful conversation together.

After the royal party left, I reached down and ate another of the delicious little blueberry muffins that were on our table. A very tall English lady, with teeth pointing east and west, stormed over and barked, "We nevah pahtake of the delicacies once the Queen Mothah has depahted."

I looked her in the eye, smiled, put another muffin in my mouth, and she angrily turned on her heels and stormed away. Staci thought that was funny, laughed, and under her breath offered a single word of insight. "Bitch." I'm sure the Queen Mother would have wanted me to have that muffin because I never met a nicer lady in my life.

One of the highlights of my life was being invited to Australia during the Melbourne Cup Festival in 1990 to speak at the National

Racehorse Dinner and also at a luncheon of the Carbine Club. Among the audience of five hundred men were the all-time top sportsmen in Australia.

Before leaving, I asked my older and wiser friend Bill Young whether I should take my guitar.

He said, "Hawk, by all means take it because they won't remember a damn thing you say, but if you take that guitar, they'll never forget you." I gave my speech about Sunday Silence and included the story about my father calling me the canary, which they loved. Then I pulled my guitar from under the table and strapped it on. I looked up and said, "Daddy, if you can hear me, the canary finally made it to Australia!" The crowd roared and I had the feeling Daddy was proud.

I closed by singing *Sunday Silence* and they all seemed to be very moved. In the end, that group of the biggest, burliest, and most rugged Australians you ever saw stood up and gave me a hearty, standing ovation.

I loved Australia and while in Melbourne, Staci and I saw a statue of the poet Adam Lindsay Gordon with the inscription:

> *"Life is mostly froth and bubble.*
> *Two things stand like stone.*
> *Kindness in another's trouble.*
> *Courage in your own."*
> —ADAM LINDSAY GORDON

Bill Young and I had some good karma with horses. In 1988, he told me his young stallion, Storm Cat, wasn't getting a lot of mares and he wondered if I'd like to foal share and breed one of my mares to him. I agreed and bred my mare Country Romance, by Halo. That mating produced a nice colt we named Harlan after a Kentucky county. Bill and I had a lot of fun racing him together, winning several races and the prestigious Vosburgh Stakes.

Storm Cat became the Leading Sire in North America eventually standing for $500,000. Harlan went on to stud at Stone Farm where he sired our homebred Menifee. The karma really kicked in when he sired Harlan's Holiday, who in turn sired Into Mischief—five times the leading sire in North America. Together, Bill and I established a new branch of the Northern Dancer sire line.

When I was only eight years old, a horse owner and friend of my parents named Jimmy Stone took me to the betting window at Keeneland and helped me make my first two-dollar bet. The horse won and I'll never forget the thrill and excitement of cashing my first ticket.

As fate would have it, years later Jimmy became a friend and good client of Stone Farm. Together, we owned that wonderful racehorse named Menifee. He was by Harlan out of my mare Anne Campbell, who went on to become Broodmare of the Year. When Menifee failed to sell at auction as a yearling at Keeneland, I asked Jimmy to be my partner.

After placing second in the Tampa Bay Derby, Menifee shipped to Kentucky to run in the prestigious Blue Grass Stakes. Here we were again back at Keeneland—all these years later! As we gathered in the saddling paddock before the race, a bird pooped on the left shoulder of my blue blazer. Jim Host was standing nearby and reached for his handkerchief to wipe it off.

I said, "Oh no, Jim. That's a sign of good luck."

Jim and his business partners laughed and thought I was half nuts, but they all placed bets anyway.

After Menifee won, I told them, "Never scoff at fate."

Menifee winning the 1999 Bluegrass Stakes at Keeneland, our favorite track – Hancock Family Photo

In the Kentucky Derby, Menifee came charging down the stretch and was second by a neck to Charismatic. Two weeks later, he was second again to that rival in the Preakness Stakes.

Jimmy Stone said, "We've come a long way since I placed that bet for you." It's amazing how things go full circle.

I am proud to look back on all the good horses we have raised at Stone Farm. The number is now more than two hundred stakes winners, and only recently we raised another Horse of the Year, Bricks and Mortar, for my long-time friend and client, George Strawbridge.

I met George in Saratoga Springs when we were young men. He was a leading steeplechase rider and has been a consummate horseman all his life. Our family relationship goes back to the time when his father and mine were roommates at Princeton.

I have always said that it is truly amazing what a good horse can do for a country bastard from Bourbon County, Kentucky.

With Olivia Newton John and Mama – Bert Morgan Photo

In my youth growing up on Claiborne Farm, I was witness to many historical happenings in the horse world. I was there with my father at the railway station in Paris when Nasrullah arrived from Ireland to begin his amazingly successful stud career in the U.S. I remember when Princequillo shipped in from our Virginia farm, Ellerslie, to begin his fabulous stud career in Kentucky.

Going with my dad to the foaling barn on April 6, 1954, I saw two colts foaled. One was Bold Ruler, a son of Nasrullah, and the other was Round Table, a son of Princequillo. Was it fate or coincidence that they were born on the same night? They both grew up to be outstanding racehorses and foundation stallions. Bold Ruler ended up siring maybe the best racehorse of all time, the great Secretariat. Round Table was an American Hall of Fame racehorse and is considered the greatest turf horse in American racing history.

With three great retired broodmares in 1970: Miss Disco, the dam of leading sire Bold Ruler, and to my left, Knight's Daughter, the dam of leading sire Round Table. Next to her is the great Grey Flight who was the dam of nine stakes winners including leading sire What a Pleasure. Miss Disco and Grey Flight were owned by the Phipps family and my father purchased Knight's Daughter from King George VI in the Royal Consignment at the December Sales in New Market, England in 1951 – John Adger Photo

Loving horses all my life as beautiful and soulful animals has always inspired me to advocate for them. The sport of kings owes its very existence to them, and it is our responsibility to treat them like the royalty they are. My dear friend, Jimmy Moseley shared these same sentiments along with a penchant for good whiskey. Over the years and during many late-night soirees hosted by Jimmy and his wife Trisha at their Saratoga home, the subject of drugs in horseracing was the hot topic. If a disagreement arose, Jimmy would suggest another "attitude adjuster" to help settle the matter and we'd pour another round until the wee hours. Jimmy would always say, "It's not so much what's wrong as whether or not you can fix it."

Looking back over the years, one of the blessings of my life was that I was exposed to so many talented artists and wonderful musicians who inspired me, brightened my life, and kept me pickin' right on to the age of 81.

Being around Peter Rowan and going with him to a few of the rehearsals of the Bluegrass Boys really inspired me to become more of a bluegrass devotee than I already was. When I came home for the Christmas break in 1964, I inquired if there was any bluegrass music in Lexington. I was told that there was a great banjo player who was playing at Martin's Place on North Limestone.

I went on a Saturday night and was amazed by him and his band. He was the best I'd ever heard other than Earl Scruggs. His name was J.D. Crowe. During the break I introduced myself to him, and he asked if I would like to get up and do a couple of numbers.

We were good friends ever since and he played banjo on my CD, *Sunday Silence.* J.D. was a legend in bluegrass music, and I followed him from all those years since the '60s and watched him inspire and put together bands with Keith Whitley, Tony Rice, Doyle Lawson, Jerry Douglas and many others. In 1975, I sat in with J.D. at The Red Slipper Lounge and a new band member sang harmony with me. He was unbelievably good. I asked J.D. why he didn't let that young boy sing more and he replied, "Because he'd get the big head." That boy turned out to be Ricky Skaggs.

Outside of Nashville, Lexington became the Mecca for bluegrass music, and it was all spearheaded and organized by J.D. Crowe. I was proud to call him my friend. I take great pleasure and pride in having seen this original art form flourish and become world famous, in no small part due to the lifelong dedication and inspirational expertise of this remarkable man.

In the studio recording my bluegrass CD, Sunday Silence. Left to Right: Stuart Ducan (fiddle), Peter Rowan (producer and vocal harmony), me (vocals and guitar), J.D. Crowe (banjo), Sam Bush (mandolin), Bill Vorndick (sound engineer), Bryan Sutton (guitar) and Mark Fain (bass) – Hancock Family Photo

Being with Fred Foster when he was inducted in the Country Music Hall of Fame in 2016 along with Charlie Daniels and Randy Travis filled me with admiration for my long-time dear friend. It was well deserved, and I couldn't have been more proud of him.

Willie Nelson's seventieth birthday was celebrated at the famous Beacon Theatre in New York City in 2003. Hearing my friend Ray Price and Willie sing a song I had co-written was indeed an honor. When they broke into *Run That by Me One More Time* at a once in a lifetime concert with some of the biggest names in music, I was floored.

One night in the early '60s, some friends and I went to The Palms Club in north Nashville to hear some country music. While the band was playing, a fight broke out on the dance floor and the lead singer jumped off of the stage, grabbed the two guys who were fighting by their collars and threw them out. When the band took their break, I found him and told him how much I admired his courage. I told him he was one of the best singers I'd ever heard and that he truly inspired me. He and I talked for a while about songs and our mutual love of music. A year or so later, I saw him on TV and recognized him. His name was Merle Haggard.

A week after graduating from Vanderbilt, I jumped in my Pontiac and traveled out West. I went to Aspen for about three weeks and while I was there, I got to hear a short-haired guy in thick round glasses singing and playing. He was a remarkably talented song-writer and musician. He introduced himself as John Deutschendorf. He was very friendly to me and gave me some great musical advice. When I heard him again seven years later on the radio, he was John Denver.

In March of 1966, when I went to work in New York, I would go into Greenwich Village where I got to hear the great folk singers Joan Baez and Dave Von Ronk several times. Later that same year, I drove north from Saratoga to Lake George, New York and happened upon the as yet undiscovered Canadian legend Gordon Lightfoot making a twelve-string guitar sound like an entire band. I couldn't get over his three-finger picking style. He was kind enough to give me a brief lesson backstage after the show. His inspiration meant the world to me.

David Cassidy and I both shared a love of Thoroughbred horses, music and Kentucky bourbon. I'll never forget the evening we sat on the porch in Saratoga with our families, singing songs and talking horses late into the night. I was amazed at his immense talent and his passion for racing. But sadly, like so many others, he made the fatal decision to keep on drinking, denying that he had a problem—until it was too late. King Alcohol destroyed another beautiful soul.

Elmo Shropshire had been a veterinarian at Belmont Park when I worked there in 1966. He and I became friends and he said he had always wanted to play the banjo but that he was too old—he was thirty. I told him he wasn't and that I would show him a few chords if he would get a banjo. That was his introduction to music.

Years later, Elmo and his wife Patsy were entertaining on a cruise ship in Alaska when they strolled over to a table of eight elderly women. When Elmo asked where they were from, they told him

Kentucky. Elmo said he had a dear friend from Paris named Arthur Hancock and wondered if any of them knew him.

One of the ladies spoke up and said, "I'm his mothah!"

Later on, he came to visit me in Kentucky, and we gave Mama a concert, which she thoroughly enjoyed. And, eventually, as fate would have it, he recorded a song called *Grandma Got Run Over by a Reindeer*, which became one of the top-selling Christmas songs of all time. He has always said that if it wasn't for me, he would still be practicing veterinary medicine.

Was it mere coincidence or destiny that I happened upon all of these inspiring musicians? My emotional reaction to hearing each of them was the same as when I heard the Carter Family on the old hand-cranked Victrola as a boy. My natural inclination is to believe in the spiritual nature of things. How many simple coincidences does it take before the words *omen* and *fate* come to mind? In the world of music and horses, I found them aplenty.

AFTERWORD

THE ANIMAL MAGNETISM of the horse and the creativity of human beings have made for a wonderful life. These stories, poems and lyrics are woven together to share the fabric of my life on my road less traveled.

When I left my birthright and what I thought was predestined as my future, my life took an unexpected turn. I had no idea what was in store for me. Much like the millions of people who boarded boats and sailed to America with no clue as to what awaited them, I believe that what often appears in human affairs under the guise of luck, chance, and coincidence is really the higher hand weaving the thread of our lives in mysterious ways. They entrusted their lives and destinies to that higher power, hoped for the best, and left the rest to him.

Like many of them, I have had several brushes with life-changing circumstances, but I survived somehow—maybe because I have always been truthful and tried to be good to people, lessons I learned early from my father who was widely known as a man of his word.

I have tried to uphold that family tradition and treat people the way I would want to be treated myself.

Fate and destiny have been kind to me. The key is to find what you like doing in life and then work like hell at it. Live your passions—and fish in the right pond with the right bait with the right people. And as my father always said, "The only real happiness in life is a job well done."

That philosophy has been my redemption, and I have tried to pass it on to my own children, who along with Staci are the lights of my life. My five daughters, Walker, Hutchi, Kate, Alex, and Lynn along with my son Arthur, have truly brightened my life. When it comes to raising children, George Strait said it best in his wonderful song:

> *"Daddies don't just love their children*
> *Every now and then*
> *It's a love without end, Amen*
> *It's a love without end, Amen"*

And without Staci, God knows where I might have ended up.

My family with me at the Thoroughbred Club of America Dinner where I was the 2020 Honor Guest
– Bill Straus Photo

EVERYTHING THAT I AM

You're my reason for living, darling, you saved my life
And I am so thankful that you are my wife
It's truly amazing the change I've been through
Everything that I am . . . I owe to you

I'm nothing without you and always would be
For all that I am is because you love me
If you ever left me, my life would be through
Everything that I am . . . I owe to you

All that I am I owe it to you
All that I've done you helped me do
They may give me the credit
But you know it's true
Everything that I am . . . I owe to you

Our beautiful children who play on our lawn
The magical mornings we've greeted the dawn
I love you and thank you for all that you do
Everything that I am . . . I owe to you

All that I am I owe it to you
All that I've done you helped me do
They may give me the credit
But you know it's true
Everything that I am . . . I owe to you
Everything that I am . . . I owe to you

IT HAS BEEN OVER FIFTY YEARS since I struck out on my own and started Stone Farm and I can say without hesitation that for all the hard work, the trials, and the highs and lows, it was worth the risk. As Goethe said, "Whatever you can do, or dream you can, begin it. Boldness has genius, power, and magic in it. Begin it now."

Sometimes your bad luck is your good luck. Not being wanted by the advisors at Claiborne turned out to be the best thing ever for me. Had I stayed there and licked their boots, there's no telling what would have become of me.

DARLIN' THANK YOU

Darlin', thank you for walkin' out on me
Even though it broke my heart at the time
Darlin', thank you for settin' me free
It's the nicest thing that anyone has ever done for me.

One of the main reasons I wrote this book is because if it helps change the life of just one person for the better, it will have been worth the effort. One night of what they thought would be frolic and fun has resulted in thousands of people becoming invalids. Thousands more are in prison for having done something terrible they may not even remember—all because of one dark night of over-indulging. Many others are living broken and ruined lives because of the consequences of their association with what they thought was their best friend, ethyl alcohol. Their celebrations and attempts to ease their cares and heartaches have become their living nightmares, while others haven't survived.

So, I hope sharing my story may help that one person. As Ian Anderson sang in his song, *Wond'ring Aloud,* "*It's only the giving that makes you what you are.*" And, as Grandpa Jones wrote in *Falling Leaves,* "*When you leave this world for a better home some day, the only thing you'll take is what you gave away.*"

After his brilliant racing career, the dark horse Sunday Silence went on to become one of the leading sires in the world, putting Japanese breeding at the pinnacle internationally. His bloodline has proven to be second to none. Only recently, his son Deep Impact sired the winner of the English and Irish Derbies, while some of his other grandsons have been knocking on the door of the Kentucky Derby.

Sunday Silence died in 2002 at the age of sixteen having been one of the finest racehorses and stallions this world has ever seen.

As the other dark horse, I am nearing the finish line. It has been a good run. I haven't had a drink in 37 years. Making that choice and leaving Claiborne changed the path of my life. Those were the best decisions I ever made.

Trying my best to do the next right thing and working hard, I have been rewarded with miracle after miracle. As Christopher Morley wrote, "There is only one success—to be able to spend your life in your own way." Onward and upward!

TIME OLD FAITHFUL FRIEND OF MINE

Watch the tiny children play
They don't really know what they are facing
See them laugh and run away, but running swifter
Through each day that's racing
Time, time, old faithful friend of mine

When my first love left me here
Alone crying and filled with fear you moved me
You took me riding through the years
Left behind my grief and tears and soothed me
Time, time, old faithful friend of mine

Time, with the seasons you have flown
Your years have gently aged the wine
You've helped me harvest seeds that I have sown
Time, time, old faithful friend of mine

So when the problems cloud your mind
And you long to leave behind your grieving
If you can only wait you'll find
With the clouds old father time is leaving
Time, time, old faithful friend of mine

Sunday Silence – J.Fukuda Photo

Acknowledgments

WRITING THIS BOOK has proved to be a long, cathartic journey. Over the course of the last 30 years my friend, John Adger and others urged me to put my story on paper. I got further encouragement from tiptop writers in their own right—Ken Tomlinson, Bill Nack, and Lenny Shulman.

But it was Jim Squires who convinced me that I could write my own book and tell my own story. He said he would guide me and be my editor. So that is how the book was born.

I am grateful to wordsmith Chris McGrath for his wise counsel, and to Ruthie Bowen for her meticulous attention to detail. Thank you to Bethany Brown at The Cadence Group and Gwyn Flowers at GKS Creative.

I would like to express my deepest appreciation to my children, Walker, Hutchi, Kate, Alex, Arthur, and Lynn, for their encouragement and input, as well as my friends Melissa and Paul Sullivan, Marshall Chapman, and Castor Fernandez. My very special thanks goes to my wife, Staci, who has helped me persevere for four long years of working on this manuscript.

They all gave me good advice about telling my story, which is illustrated with the images from some great photographers and brought to life by the photographic expertise of Bobby Shiflet and Steven Beaven.

Thank you all—I couldn't have done it without you.

Songs and Poems Index

www.ingramcontent.com/pod-product-compliance
Lightning Source LLC
Chambersburg PA
CBHW041303120726
48005CB00014B/1847